PEROVSKITE NANOSTRUCTURE BASED ELECTROCHEMICAL BIOSENSOR FOR SELECTIVE DETERMINATION OF DOPAMINE

APARNA T K

TABLE OF CONTENTS

CHAPTER NO.	TITLE	PAGE NO.
	ABSTRACT	iii
	LIST OF TABLES	x
	LIST OF FIGURES	xi
	LIST OF SYMBOLS AND ABBREVIATIONS	xviii
1	**INTRODUCTION**	1
1.1	BACKGROUND	1
	1.1.1 Neurotransmitters	1
	1.1.2 Dopamine	2
	1.1.3 Importance of DA Detection	3
	1.1.4 Electrochemical Biosensors	4
1.2	ROLE OF NANOMATERIALS IN BIOSENSORS	7
1.3	SCOPE OF THE PRESENT WORK	7
1.4	OBJECTIVES	8
1.5	OUTLINE OF THE THESIS	9
2	**REVIEW OF LITERATURE**	11
2.1	METHODS FOR DA DETECTION	11
2.2	ELECTROCHEMICAL METHOD	16
	2.2.1 Electrochemical Cell	16
	2.2.2 Different Electrochemical Techniques	18
2.3	ELECTROCHEMICAL METHOD FOR DA DETECTION	23
	2.3.1 Electrochemistry of DA	24
2.4	NANOMATERIALS FOR ELECTROCHEMICAL SENSING OF DA	25

CHAPTER NO.	TITLE	PAGE NO.

		2.4.1 Metal Nanoparticles	25
		2.4.2 Metal Oxide Nanoparticles	27
		2.4.3 Core-shell Nanostructures	29
		2.4.4 CNT based nanocomposite	31
		2.4.5 Mixed Metal Oxides	33
		2.4.5.1 Spinels	33
		2.4.5.2 Perovskites	35
	2.5	CHALLENGES IN DA DETECTION AND MOTIVATION OF THE WORK	39
	2.6	SUMMARY	40
3		$FeTiO_3$ NANOHEXAGONS BASED ELECTROCHEMICAL SENSOR FOR THE DETECTION OF DOPAMINE	42
	3.1	INTRODUCTION	42
	3.2	MATERIALS AND METHODS	43
		3.2.1 Chemicals	43
		3.2.2 Synthesis of $FeTiO_3$ nanohexagons	43
		3.2.3 Material Characterization	44
		3.2.4 Electrochemical Measurements	44
		3.2.5 Analysis of Real Samples	45
	3.3	RESULTS AND DISCUSSION	45
		3.3.1 Characterization of $FeTiO_3$	45
		3.3.1.1 Morphological characterization of $FeTiO_3$	45
		3.3.1.2 XRD and FTIR Analysis	47
		3.3.1.3 XPS analysis of $FeTiO_3$	48
		3.3.1.4 Nitrogen Adsorption/Desorption Studies of $FeTiO_3$	49
		3.3.1.5 EIS spectrum of $FeTiO_3$	50

CHAPTER NO.	TITLE	PAGE NO.

		3.3.2	Electro-oxidation of DA on FeTiO$_3$/GCE	51
		3.3.3	Calculation of Number of Electrons Transferred (n) and Catalytic Rate Constant (k$_{cat}$)	53
		3.3.4	pH Dependent Sensing of DA on FeTiO$_3$/GCE	54
		3.3.5	DPV Analysis	55
		3.3.6	Selective and Simultaneous Detection of DA and UA	57
		3.3.7	Stability and Reproducibility Studies	60
		3.3.8	Estimation of DA and UA in Human Biological Samples	61
	3.4	SUMMARY		61
4	STUDIES ON THE ELECTROCHEMISTRY OF DOPAMINE ON FeTiO$_3$ MODIFIED GLASSY CARBON ELECTRODE			63
	4.1	INTRODUCTION		63
	4.2	MATERIALS AND METHODS		64
		4.2.1	Synthesis of FeTiO$_3$ Nanohexagons	64
		4.2.2	Electrochemical Measurements	64
	4.3	RESULTS AND DISCUSSION		64
		4.3.1	Electrochemical behaviour of DA on FeTiO$_3$/GCE	64
		4.3.2	Effect of pH on Redox Reaction of DA	69
		4.3.3	Hydrodynamic Voltammetry	71
		4.3.4	Impedance Studies	72
		4.3.5	Comparison with GCE	75
	4.4	SUMMARY		76

CHAPTER NO.	TITLE	PAGE NO.

5 POLYDOPAMINE COATED FeTiO$_3$ NANOHEXAGONS FOR ELECTROCHEMICAL DETECTION OF DOPAMINE   78

- 5.1 INTRODUCTION   78
- 5.2 MATERIALS AND METHODS   79
  - 5.2.1 Synthesis of FeTiO$_3$ Nanohexagons   79
  - 5.2.2 Synthesis of PDA Coated FeTiO$_3$ Nanocomposite   79
  - 5.2.3 Preparation of DA Stock Solutions and Real Samples   79
  - 5.2.4 Electrochemical Measurements   80
- 5.3 RESULTS AND DISCUSSION   80
  - 5.3.1 Characterization of PDA-FeTiO$_3$ 80
    - 5.3.1.1 SEM   80
    - 5.3.1.2 TEM   82
    - 5.3.1.3 XRD   84
    - 5.3.1.4 FTIR   85
    - 5.3.1.5 XPS   86
    - 5.3.1.6 EIS Spectroscopy   87
  - 5.3.2 Electrocatalytic Activity of PDA-FeTiO$_3$/GCE   88
  - 5.3.3 pH Study   90
  - 5.3.4 Sensing of DA and UA   91
  - 5.3.5 Selective and Simultaneous Detection of DA and UA   93
  - 5.3.6 Real Sample Analysis   97
- 5.4 SUMMARY   97

CHAPTER NO.	TITLE	PAGE NO.
6	**CONCLUSIONS AND FUTURE SCOPE**	**99**
	6.1 FUTURE PERSPECTIVES	100
	REFERENCES	**102**
	LIST OF PUBLICATIONS	**122**

LIST OF TABLES

TABLE NO.	TITLE	PAGE NO.
2.1	Performance of Metal Oxides Modified Electrodes In DA Sensing	28
2.2	Performance of Perovskites in the Electrochemical Detection of H_2O_2, Glucose and DA	39
3.1	A Comparative Performance of Various Perovskite Modified Electrode for DA Sensing	57
3.2	DA and UA Estimation in Human Biological Samples using $FeTiO_3$/GCE	61
4.1	Peak Potential Separation and Peak Current Ratio for 0.5 mM DA at pH 7 at Different Scan Rate	68
4.2	Redox Potentials and Peak Currents Estimated from Cyclic Voltammetry at Different pH	70
4.3	EEC Parameters at Different Applied Potential for $FeTiO_3$/GCE	74
5.1	A Comparative Performance of Various Polymer based DA Biosensors	93
5.2	DA and UA Estimation in Human Biological Samples using PDA-$FeTiO_3$/GCE	97

LIST OF FIGURES

FIGURE NO.	TITLE	PAGE NO.
1.1	Molecular Structures of Various Neurotransmitters	1
1.2	Structure of DA	3
1.3	Schematic Diagram showing the Components of an Electrochemical Biosensor	5
1.4	Scheme for the Oxidation Pathway of DA. Steps 1,2,3,4 Correspond to ECE and Steps 1,2,3,5 Depicts to ECC Mechanism Respectively	6
2.1	Schematic Representation for Colorimetric Detection of DA using Au NPs	12
2.2	Schematic Representation of an Electrochemiluminescence Sensor based on GSH-Ag/Au NCs for Detection of DA	13
2.3	Schematic Representation of an Electrochemical cell	17
2.4	(a) Excitation Waveform and (b) Typical Response of CV	18
2.5	(a) Excitation Waveform and (b) Typical Response of DPV	19
2.6	(a) Excitation Waveform and (b) Typical Response of Chronoamperometry	20
2.7	(a) Excitation Waveform and (b) Typical Response of EIS	21
2.8	(a) Excitation Waveform and (b) Typical Response of Rotating disk Voltammetry	22

FIGURE NO.	TITLE	PAGE NO.
2.9	Schematic Representation for Electrochemical Detection of DA using Metal Nanoparticles based Composite	26
2.10	Schematic Representation for Electrochemical Detection of DA and PA using Core-shell Nanostructure	30
2.11	Electrochemical Detection of DA using CNT based Nanocomposite	32
2.12	Structure of AB_2X_4 Spinel	34
2.13	Spinel Structure for Electrochemical Detection of DA	35
2.14	Structure of ABO_3 Perovskite	36
2.15	Schematic Representation for Electrochemical Detection of DA using Perovskite Nanostructure	38
3.1	(a-c) TEM Images of $FeTiO_3$ Recorded at Different Magnifications; (d) the Corresponding SAED Pattern and (e) shows the EDX Image Respectively	46
3.2	(a) XRD Pattern and (b) FTIR Spectrum of $FeTiO_3$ Nanostructure and the Inset shows the Expanded View in the Region between 3500 cm^{-1} to 1000 cm^{-1}	47
3.3	XPS Spectrum of $FeTiO_3$ (a) Survey Spectrum, (b) Fe 2p, (c) O 1s and (d) Ti 2p Respectively	48
3.4	Nitrogen Adsorption/Desorption Isotherm Curves of $FeTiO_3$ Nanostructures and the Inset Depicts the Pore Size Distribution	49

FIGURE NO.	TITLE	PAGE NO.
3.5	Nyquist Plot for Bare GCE and FeTiO$_3$/GCE Recorded from a Solution of 0.1 M PBS and 5 mM K$_4$[Fe(CN)$_6$] in the Frequency Range of 10^6 Hz to 0.01 Hz	50
3.6	Electrooxidation of DA on FeTiO$_3$	51
3.7	Cyclic Voltammogramm Depicting the Response of DA on FeTiO$_3$/GCE from a Solution of 0.1 M PBS and 0.1 mM of DA at a Scan Rate of 100 mV s^{-1}. The Inset Depicts the Response of bare GCE under Identical Condition	52
3.8	(a) CV Response of FeTiO$_3$/GCE for 0.1 mM DA at Different Scan Rates and (b) the Corresponding Calibration Plot	53
3.9	(a) CA Response of FeTiO$_3$/GCE in the Presence and Absence of DA at an Applied Potential of 0.15 V and (b) Depicts the Plot between t$^{1/2}$ vs I$_{cat}$/I$_L$	54
3.10	(a) DPV Response for DA on FeTiO$_3$/GCE at a pH Range of 4 to 9 from a 0.1 M PBS Solution and (b) the Variation of E$_{pa}$ and I$_{pa}$ with Respect to pH	55
3.11	DPV Curves for (a) DA (1 µM to 350 µM) and (c) UA (1 µM to 500 µM) on FeTiO$_3$/GCE from a Solution of 0.1 M PBS, (b)&(d) shows the Corresponding Calibration Plot	56
3.12	(a) DPV Response of DA in Presence of Various Concentration of UA (50 µM to 250 µM) and (b) their Corresponding Calibration Curve	58

FIGURE NO.	TITLE	PAGE NO.
3.13	(a) DPV Response for Simultaneous Detection of DA and UA for Various Concentrations on FeTiO$_3$/GCE in 0.1 M PBS and (b) & (c) their Corresponding Calibration Plots	59
3.14	(a) Bar Plot Depicting the Variation of Peak Current for DA Detection in Presence of Various Interfering Agents and (b) the CV Response of 0.1 mM DA for the 1st and 75th Cycle	60
4.1	Cyclic Voltammogram Depicting the First and Second Cycle Obtained for the Redox Reaction of 0.5 mM DA in 0.1 M PBS at a Scan Rate of 50 mV s^{-1}	65
4.2	(a) Cyclic Voltmmograms Obtained for the Redox Reaction of 0.5 mM DA in 0.1 M PBS at Different Scan Rate from 100 mV s^{-1} to 500 mV s^{-1}; (b) the Corresponding Plot between Peak Current vs $v^{½}$ and (c) Plot between ln (v) vs Peak Potential	66
4.3	CV Corresponding to the Redox Reaction of DA on FeTiO$_3$/GCE at Scan Rate Ranging from 10 mV s^{-1} to 50 mV s^{-1}	67
4.4	(a) CV Curves Recorded for the Redox Reaction of DA at Different pH and (b) the Plot between Formal Potential (E$^{o'}$) vs pH	70
4.5	(a) CV Recorded for the Redox Reaction of DA for 25 Continuous Cycles from a Solution of 0.5 mM of DA and 0.1 M PBS at a Scan Rate of 50 mV s^{-1} and (b) ATR-FTIR Studies of Polydopamine Formation on Bare GCE and FeTiO$_3$/GCE	71

FIGURE NO.	TITLE	PAGE NO.
4.6	(a) RDE Curves Recorded at Different Rotation Rates for the Oxidation of 0.5 mM DA in 0.1 M PBS in the Potential Range of -0.2 V to 0.8 V at a Scan of 50 mV s^{-1} and (b) their K-L Plot	72
4.7	(a) Nyquist Plot Obtained for the Oxidation of DA at Different Applied Potentials; the Inset Depicts the Plot Obtained for Blank Solution (0.1 M PBS alone) at their OCP and (b) the Corresponding Electrical Equivalent Circuit	73
4.8	Bode Plot (a) log (f) vs Phase Angle and (b) Log (f) vs |z| for the Oxidation of DA at Different Applied Potential on FeTiO$_3$/GCE	75
4.9	(a) CV Corresponding to the Redox Reaction of DA on Bare GCE at Scan Rate Ranging from 100 mV s^{-1} to 500 mV s^{-1} and (b) the Corresponding Plot between i$_p$ vs v^{½}	76
5.1	(a and b) FESEM Images of FeTiO$_3$ Recorded at Different Magnifications; (c and d) FESEM Images of PDA-FeTiO$_3$ Recorded at Different Magnifications	81
5.2	(a) Elemental Map showing the Distribution of Different Elements in FeTiO$_3$ Nanostructure; (b, c and d) Elemental Maps showing Individual Elements Fe, Ti and O Respectively	81
5.3	(a) Elemental Map showing the Distribution of Different Elements in PDA-FeTiO$_3$ Nanocomposite; (b, c and d) Elemental Maps showing Individual Elements Fe, Ti and O Respectively	82

FIGURE NO.	TITLE	PAGE NO.
5.4	(a-d) TEM Images of FeTiO$_3$ Recorded at Different Magnifications; (d) the Corresponding SAED Pattern and (e) shows the EDX Image Respectively	83
5.5	XRD Pattern of FeTiO$_3$ and PDA-FeTiO$_3$ Nanocomposite	84
5.6	FTIR Spectrum of FeTiO$_3$ and PDA-FeTiO$_3$ Nanocomposite	85
5.7	XPS Spectrum of PDA-FeTiO$_3$ (a) Survey Spectrum, (b) Fe 2p, (c) O 1s, (d) Ti 2p, (e) C 1s and (f) N 1s Respectively	86
5.8	Nyquist Plot for FeTiO$_3$/GCE and PDA-FeTiO$_3$/GCE Recorded from a Solution of 0.1 M PBS and 5 mM K$_4$[Fe(CN)$_6$] in the Frequency Range of 10^6 Hz to 1 Hz	88
5.9	Cyclic Voltammogramm Depicting the Response of DA on FeTiO$_3$/GCE and PDA-FeTiO$_3$/GCE from a Solution of 0.1 M PBS and 0.1 mM of DA at a Scan Rate of 100 mV s^{-1}	89
5.10	(a) CV Response of PDA-FeTiO$_3$/GCE for 0.1 mM DA at Different Scan Rates and (b) the Corresponding Calibration Plot	90
5.11	(a) CV Curves for 0.1 mM DA on PDA-FeTiO$_3$/GCE at a pH Range of 3 to 11 from a 0.1 M PBS Solution and (b) the Variation of E$_{pa}$ and I$_{pa}$ with Respect to pH	91

FIGURE NO.	TITLE	PAGE NO.
5.12	DPV Curves for (a) DA (50 μM to 250 μM) and (c) UA (50 μM to 250 μM) on PDA-FeTiO$_3$/GCE from a Solution of 0.1 M PBS and (b), (d) shows the Corresponding Calibration Plot	92
5.13	DPV Responses on PDA-FeTiO$_3$/GCE in 0.1 M PBS at Different Concentrations of (a) DA (100 μM to 500 μM), (c) UA (100 μM to 500 μM) and (b, d) their Corresponding Calibration Curves	94
5.14	(a) DPV Response for Simultaneous Detection of DA and UA for Various Concentrations on PDA-FeTiO$_3$/GCE in 0.1 M PBS and (b) & (c) their Corresponding Calibration Plots	95
5.15	Bar Plot Depicting the Variation of Peak Current for DA Detection in Presence of Various Interfering Agents	96

CHAPTER 1

INTRODUCTION

1.1 BACKGROUND

1.1.1 Neurotransmitters

Neurotransmitters are chemical messengers in the brain (Graybiel *et al*. 1990). The nervous system, using these neurotransmitters transmits information to the muscles and other parts of the body. Synaptic cleft, the small gap between synapses of neurons is where the communication between two neurons occurs. Electrical signals along the axon are converted to chemical signals by the release of neurotransmitters, which cause a specific response in the receiving neuron.

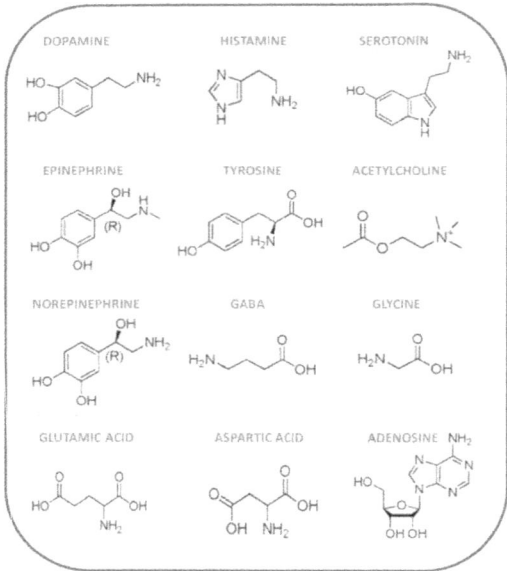

Figure 1.1. Molecular Structures of Various Neurotransmitters

Neurotransmitters can be amines, amino acids or neuropeptides (Webster *et al.* 2001). These neurotransmitters and their interactions are involved in various functions of the nervous system. Some of the important neurotransmitters are shown in Figure 1.1 such as acetylcholine, glutamate, aspartic acid, γ-aminobutyric acid (GABA), glycine, dopamine, epinephrine, noradrenaline (norepinephrine), serotonin, tyrosine, adenosine and histamine (Griffith *et al.* 1982, Hadjiconstantinou *et al.* 1983, Schwartz *et al.* 1980, Bowery *et al.* 2006).

Neurotransmitters can either be excitatory, inhibitory or modulatory. An excitatory neurotransmitter generates an electrical signal (action potential) in the receiving neuron, whereas an inhibitory neurotransmitter prevents it. The classification of the neurotransmitter as excitatory or inhibitory depends on the receptor to which it binds (Chan *et al.* 1979, McCormick *et al.* 1989). Neuromodulators are quite different, as they are not only restricted to synaptic cleft but also affect large number of neurons at once. Neuromodulators are known to regulate the neurons (Noudoost *et al.* 2011).

1.1.2 Dopamine

DA (3,4-dihydroxyphenethylamine) is an important catecholamine neurotransmitter which is of major interest and has role in many functions such as motor control, motivation, reward and reinforcement (Dalley *et al.* 2012). DA has a catechol structure in which an amine group is attached via an ethyl chain as shown in Figure 1.2.

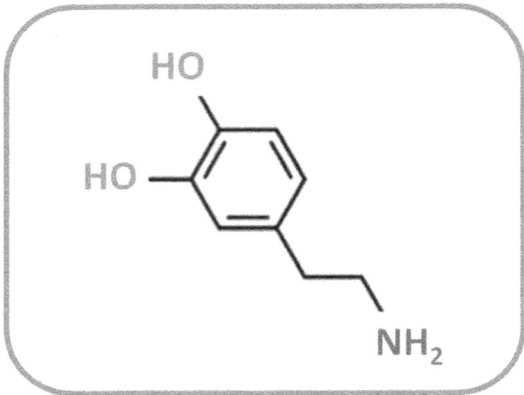

Figure 1.2. Structure of DA

The ideal concentration of DA in human body is in the range of about 10^{-6} M to 10^{-8} M. DA is formed mostly by the removal of carboxyl group from its precursor molecule L-DOPA, synthesized in brain and kidneys. DA is produced in the region of midbrain called *Substantia nigra* which is a tiny strip of tissue that is present on either side of the basal brain (Cheramy *et al*. 1981). DA is also produced in the ventral segmental area of the brain.

1.1.3 Importance of DA Detection

Body movements, muscle control and speech are controlled by DA from *Substantia nigra* (Bohnen *et al*. 2006). Death of brain cells in this region leads to low DA production. As a result, uncontrollable tremors occur which is one of the symptoms of Parkinson's disease. Parkinson's disease is a neurodegenerative progressive disorder that occurs in patients with 80 percent or greater loss of cells that produce DA (Zucca *et al*. 2017). The disease generally affects people in the age of 55 to 60, but it may also affect people who are in their early 30s. Few most common symptoms of this disorder are tremor, involuntary movements of hands and legs, decreased facial expression, muscle rigidity, decreased blinking, depression, unsteadiness in walk, drooling etc.

(Menza *et al.* 1993, Politis *et al.* 2010, Sveinbjornsdottir *et al.* 2016). Another chronic disorder that is associated with altered DA levels is Schizophrenia (Weinstein *et al.* 2017). It is a mental disorder in which the affected person shows psychotic behaviours. The symptoms include hallucination, disordered body movements, inability to speak, lack of pleasure etc. (Szendi *et al.* 2006,). Alzheimer's disease is another major disorder that is related with DA concentration (Palmer *et al.* 1993). A person affected with Alzheimer's loses his complete memory and exhibits unpredictable behaviour (Reisberg *et al.* 1987, Lyketsos *et al.* 2011). It is estimated that people above the age of 65 suffer from this disease.

It is important to monitor the concentration of neurotransmitters such as DA for the overall well-being to screen out disorders like Parkinson's disease, Schizophrenia, Alzheimer's etc. Research on DA detection is being actively pursued using several detection methods such as chromatography (Guan *et al.* 2000), mass spectrometry (Iftikhar *et al.* 2017), colorimetry (Zhang *et al.* 2017), fluorescence spectroscopy (Chen and Wang *et al.* 2018), chemiluminescence (Wang *et al.* 2018), electrophoresis etc. (Zhang *et al.* 2003). However they are time consuming, requires extreme sample preparation and specialized lab equipments whereas, electrochemical methods are simplest with fast response time and easy experimental conditions. On the other hand, DA is an electroactive compound and hence it can be easily detected by electrochemical method.

1.1.4 Electrochemical Biosensors

Biosensors are devices that are used for the measurement of an analyte of biological importance either qualitatively or quantitatively (Kissinger *et al.* 2005). Electrochemical biosensor records the response of the analyte in terms of current or voltage (Magner *et al.* 1998, Wang *et al.* 2005, Thévenot *et al.* 2001, Ronkainen *et al.* 2010, Pohanka *et al.* 2008). The electrochemical interaction of the analyte-electrode is transformed into a measurable output.

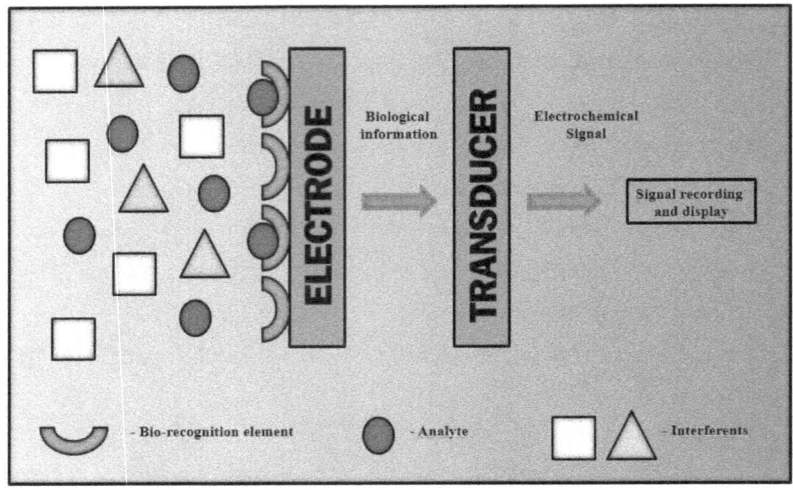

Figure 1.3. Schematic Diagram showing the Components of an Electrochemical Biosensor

Figure 1.3 shows the three main components of an electrochemical biosensor (1) the bio-recognition element responds to the analyte in solution, (2) the transducer is responsible for transformation of the signal produced from biological interaction into electrochemical signal which can be easily measured and (3) signal processors to record and display the result. Electrochemical biosensors are of two main types namely potentiometric and amperometric biosensors. Potentiometric biosensor measures the potential with respect to change in ion concentration using ion selective electrodes (Karyakin et al. 1996, Koncki et al. 2007). Amperometric biosensors are used for measurement of electric current produced as a result of electron flow from redox reactions. Amperometric biosensors are most popular compared to potentiometric, owing to their simplicity, accuracy, ease of production and cost-effectiveness of the devices (Hendry et al. 1990, Habermüller et al. 2000). They also offer numerous advantages such as small size, high surface area, and enhanced electron transfer rate. The biomolecules can be easily immobilized on the electrode surface.

The underlying basis of the electrochemical detection of DA is 2e⁻/2H⁺ redox reactions. DA is quantified by measuring the currents generated in the redox reaction as a function of their concentration. The redox current is linearly proportional to the concentration of DA.

To discuss briefly the oxidation pathway of DA as given in Figure 1.4, it undergoes a 2e⁻/2H⁺ process to form DQH which is followed by deprotonation and then intracyclization occurs to form LDC (Hawley *et al*. 1967 and Schindler *et al*. 2019). Two pathways for DA oxidation namely ECE (steps 1 to 4) and ECC (steps 1,2,3 and 5) were reported. If the LDC oxidizes to DC, then it is ECE pathway, or if it reacts with DQH to form DA and DC, then it follows a ECC pathway. However the exact mechanism for DA oxidation is still not clear.

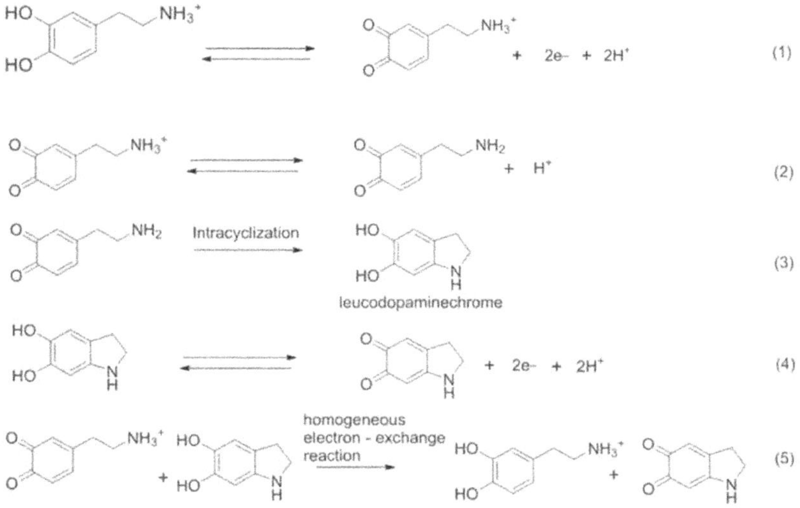

Figure 1.4. Scheme for the Oxidation Pathway of DA. Steps 1,2,3,4 Correspond to ECE and Steps 1,2,3,5 Depicts to ECC Mechanism Respectively

1.2 ROLE OF NANOMATERIALS IN BIOSENSORS

Tremendous research has been carried out in the development of novel nanomaterials for biosensing applications (Holzinger *et al.* 2014). The nanomaterials used in the electrochemical biosensors must be biocompatible and also have a large affinity towards adsorption of biomolecules. The nanomaterials are classified on the basis of their structure as (a) 0D e.g. quantum dots, (b) 1D e.g. nanorods, (c) 2D e.g. graphene sheets and (d) 3D e.g. metal organic frameworks (Gogia *et al.* 2019 and Mishra *et al.* 2017). Nanomaterials can enhance the performance of the sensor in terms of selectivity, stability, sensitivity and reproducibility (Kawasaki *et al.* 2018). The nanomaterials are used as a support material for loading biomolecules such as enzymes, antibody etc. and several other metal ions and mediators. In some cases, they are used as mimic enzyme to electrocatalyze many catalytic reactions. Metal nanoparticles, metal oxides, polymers, carbon based composites, alloys, core@shell nanostructures, 2D layered materials, perovskite nanostructures, metal/metal oxide nanocomposites are some of the nanomaterials employed in electrochemical sensing of DA (Yusoff *et al.* 2015, Khan *et al.* 2016, Huang *et al.* 2019, Li *et al.* 2012, Ramakrishnan *et al.* 2015, Zeng *et al.* 2013, Yan *et al.* 2008). A recent review emphasized the importance of nanomaterial in the electrochemical detection of DA (Chen *et al.* 2013).

1.3 SCOPE OF THE PRESENT WORK

The scope of the present work is to develop an electrochemical biosensor based on perovskite nanomaterials. Perovskites are complex oxides that have a cubic structure with general formula of ABO_3 (Li *et al.* 2004). The A site is occupied by a cation which is a larger rare earth metal, the cation in B site is a smaller transition metal and O is the oxygen anion. Perovskites are widely used in the field of Solid Oxide Fuel Cells (SOFC), solar cells, batteries etc. owing to their superior physical and chemical properties (Tao *et al.* 2003 and

Hardin *et al.* 2013). However, the material has not been explored much for sensor applications. Some of the perovskite nanostructures that are reported in literature for DA sensing are LaFeO$_3$ (Thirumalairajan *et al.* 2014), SrPdO$_3$ (Atta *et al.* 2013) and LaCoO$_3$ (Priyatharshni *et al.* 2017). In this work, a semiconductor perovskite-FeTiO$_3$ was reported for the first time in electrochemical sensing of DA. FeTiO$_3$ has a wide band gap ranging between 2.58 eV to 2.90 eV and has been employed in several applications such as catalysis, spintronics etc. (Truong *et al.* 2012, Kim *et al.* 2009 and Ribeiro *et al.* 2015). The synthesis of FeTiO$_3$ was carried out using a facile hydrothermal method excluding the use of any structure directing agents. The electrochemical kinetics of FeTiO$_3$ and the oxidation mechanism of DA on FeTiO$_3$ was studied briefly. Further to improve the stability, PDA coated FeTiO$_3$ was synthesized and its electrocatalytic activity for DA oxidation was investigated in the presence of the interfering agents. The sensor was also tested for its practical applicability in human biological serum and urine samples. The perovskite sensor could be used as a clinical biomarker for diagnosis of neurological disorders with high sensitivity and selectivity.

1.4 OBJECTIVES

The major objective of the research work is to develop a biosensor based on FeTiO$_3$ nanostructure for selective and sensitive electrochemical detection of DA. Some of the specific objectives are given below.

1. To prepare shape controlled FeTiO$_3$ perovskite nanostructure by adjusting the solution pH and reaction temperature.
2. To develop a biosensor using FeTiO$_3$ perovskite nanostructure for detecting DA electrochemically.
3. To study the electrochemistry of DA on FeTiO$_3$ modified GCE surface.
4. To synthesize PDA coated FeTiO$_3$ and develop a biosensor based on PDA- FeTiO$_3$/GCE for electrochemical detection of DA for improved selectivity and sensitivity.

1.5 OUTLINE OF THE THESIS

The main focus of the thesis is to develop an electrochemical biosensor based on perovskite nanostructure. A simple and cost effective hydrothermal method for FeTiO$_3$ perovskite synthesis without any structure directing agents was reported. In addition to this, synthesis of composite nanostructure containing PDA polymer was also prepared by a polymerization process using tris buffer solution. The electrocatalytic activity of FeTiO$_3$ and PDA- FeTiO$_3$ towards DA and the detection was studied using several electrochemical techniques. The entire thesis consists of 6 main chapters including this, which are as follows.

Chapter 2 elaborates on the literature reports pertaining to DA detection by different methods and materials. Various nanomaterials employed for DA detection and their efficacy for DA detection were discussed in detail. The basic mechanism for electrochemical DA detection and the importance of DA research was demonstrated by discussing the research communications available in recent years. Several aspects on how to increase the efficiency of sensor through parameters such as detection limit, selectivity, sensitivity, reproducibility and stability were pointed out briefly.

Chapter 3 deals with the development of an electrochemical biosensor based on FeTiO$_3$/GCE for DA detection. Some of the topics that are covered under this chapter are synthesis of FeTiO$_3$ perovskite, characterization, studies on electro-oxidation of DA on FeTiO$_3$ modified GCE (FeTiO$_3$/GCE), pH dependent DA sensing, DA detection by DPV analysis, selective and simultaneous detection of DA in presence of UA etc. The LOD was calculated for DA and UA and the sensor performance was compared with the earlier reported perovskite based electrochemical biosensors.

Chapter 4 represents the studies of DA electrochemistry on FeTiO$_3$/GCE. The electron transfer kinetics of bare GCE and FeTiO$_3$/GCE was compared. The electrochemical kinetic parameters were calculated from hydrodynamic voltammetry and impedance studies. Further, the mechanistic pathway for DA oxidation on FeTiO$_3$/GCE was proposed.

Chapter 5 explains the synthesis of PDA coated FeTiO$_3$ and the electrocatalytic activity of PDA-FeTiO$_3$/GCE for DA and UA detection. The PDA-FeTiO$_3$/GCE was synthesized by polymerization of DA in tris buffer and the material was characterized by different techniques. The performance of the sensor was studied and validated in presence of human biological serum sample.

Chapter 6 gives the conclusion and future scope of the research work.

11

CHAPTER 2

REVIEW OF LITERATURE

A detailed literature review on the electrochemical detection of DA using various materials is presented in this chapter. The chapter also gives a brief introduction about the basics of electrochemical techniques used in the sensing of analytes.

As mentioned earlier in Chapter 1, the detection of DA has garnered much interest and different techniques have been exploited in this context. To name a few, colorimetry, HPLC, ECL, fluorescence, electrochemical method, capillary electrophoresis is available for the determination of DA. The techniques will be discussed briefly, citing research literatures from the past 5 years and the advantage of electrochemical method over other methods will be highlighted. The electrochemical detection of DA by diverse nanomaterials will be discussed and the parameters such as limit of detection and linear range for DA will be specified.

2.1   METHODS FOR DA DETECTION

The detection/estimation of DA was carried out using several methods which are briefly described below.

Colorimetry is the most common method for analysis of DA which is carried out by a visually observable color change. A general schematic representation of colorimetric detection of DA is given in Figure 2.1.

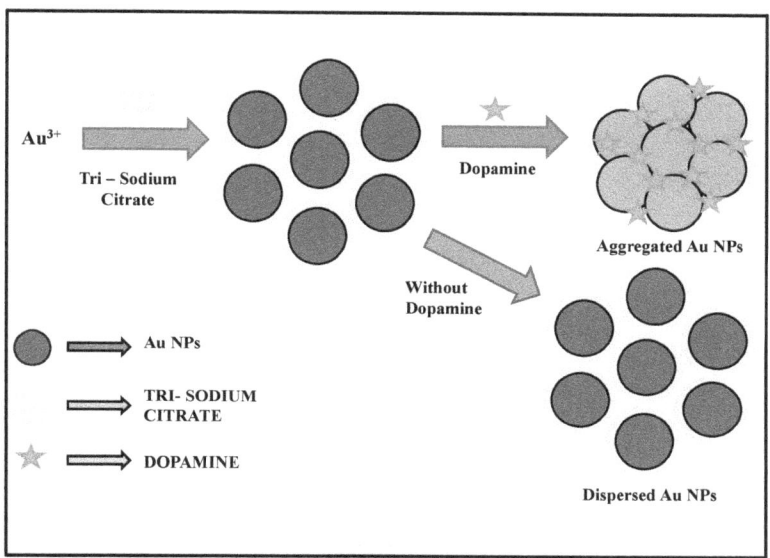

Figure 2.1. Schematic Representation for Colorimetric Detection of DA using Au NPs

Colorimetry does not require any robust instrumentation and is cost effective. However, colorimetric sensing is limited because of its low sensitivity and selectivity. A colorimetric probe was reported for the detection of DA using gold nanoparticles on the basis of interaction between DA and melamine (Chen *et al.* 2015). The melamine induced aggregation of gold nanoparticles produced a color change from red to blue, whereas in the presence of DA, a reverse color change from blue to red was observed. The nanoprobe showed a LOD of 33 nM. The determination of DA in human serum sample was also demonstrated with recovery values ranging from 90.1 % to 103.3 %. In another study, a gel based approach was used to design hierarchical CuS decorated reduced graphene oxide (rGO) nanosheets to enhance peroxidase-like activity leading to colorimetric detection of DA (Dutta *et al.* 2015). CuS-rGO nanocomposite was synthesized using a supramolecular colorless Cu(I)-thiourea hydrogel in GO framework.

The catalytic activity of CuS-rGO was enhanced due to the synergistic covalent interaction between CuS and rGO. The nanocomposite exhibited peroxidase-like activity in which TMB was changed from colorless to blue as a result of oxidation in the presence of H_2O_2. DA was sensed by successive inhibition action of H_2O_2 for TMB oxidation. The LOD was found to be 0.48 µM and the linear range was 2 µM to 100 µM respectively.

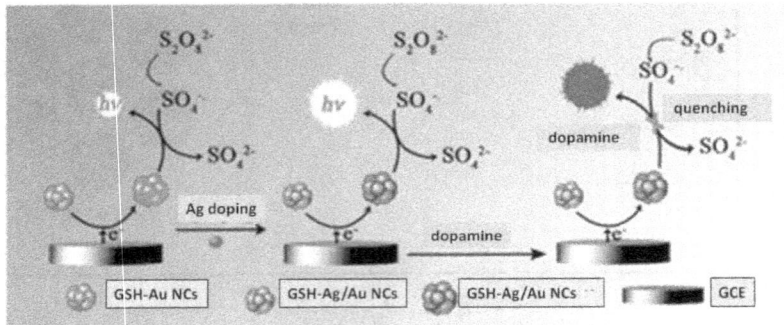

Figure 2.2. Schematic Representation of an Electrochemiluminescence Sensor based on GSH-Ag/Au NCs for Detection of DA (Tang *et al.* 2019)

ECL is of great interest owing to its advantages such as high sensitivity, low background current and rapid detection process. It works by the principle of emission of light from the excited state of the intermediate. The measure of the intensity determines the amount of DA present in the solution. Figure 2.2 shows an electrochemiluminescence sensor based on Ag doped GSH-protected Au nanoclusters. The ECL efficiency of the Au NCs was enhanced after doping and a sensor was constructed for the detection of DA. The sensor showed a LOD of 2.3 nM and a wide linear range from 10 nM to 1 mM (Tang *et al*. 2019). A dual-potential ratiometric electrochemiluminescence sensor was developed to detect DA (Fu *et al*. 2017). Graphene-CdTe quantum dots (G-CdTe QDs) was the cathodic emitter and self-enhanced Ru(II) composite

(TAEA-Ru) was the anodic emitter. The substrate used for capturing DA was APTES functionalized G-CdTe QDs. DA was captured by means of specific recognition of dihydroxy group in DA with oxyethyl group of APTES. Followed by this, Cu_2O nanocrystals supported TAEA-Ru was bound by interaction between DA amino groups and the carboxyl groups of Cu_2O- TAEA-Ru. From the ratio of ECL signals, the LOD for DA was found to be very low (2.9 fM) with a linear range from 10.0 fM to 1.0 nM. Further a chemiluminescence system based on lucigenin/thiourea dioxide was developed for selective and sensitive determination of DA (Gao *et al*. 2017). The peak intensity observed was 75 times higher compared to the familiar lucigenin/H_2O_2 system. DA suppressed the chemiluminescence of lucigenin/thiourea dioxide system. The LOD and linear range observed for DA are 14.7 nM and 20-800 nM respectively. The method also showed good selectivity for DA detection in the presence of AA, UA, amino acids and sugars.

HPLC is another versatile technique used for detection as well as the separation of individual components from complex mixtures. The technique provides high reproducibility and has been used for quality control analysis of drugs, assessment of bioequivalence, to monitor concentration of drug in blood and to quantify impurities etc. A sensitive, reproducible assay using HPLC with electrochemical method was developed for detection of monoamine neurotransmitters such as DA, norepinephrine, serotonin, their metabolites and DHBA (Allen *et al*. 2017). Chromatographic separation of biogenic amines and its relevant metabolites was achieved using C_{18} column. The linear range observed for DA was 0.300 – 30 ng/mL with LOD of 0.125 ng/mL. The sample preparation procedure used in this method was very simple and the percentage of recovery for all the analyte was ≥90 %. Online capillary liquid chromatography with electrochemical detection was reported by Gu *et al* to monitor DA *in-vivo* by microdialysis with one minute temporal resolution (Gu *et al*. 2015). The rat brain dialysate samples were analysed at one minute intervals. The optimization of the mobile phase was done by controlling the parameters such as pH, surfactant concentration and buffer composition to avoid interferences such as HVA and divalent metal ions etc. with the DA peak. The results showed that the system has bonafide sub-1 minute temporal resolution from the analysis of electrically evoked DA transients.

In the case of **Fluorescence method**, a series of fluorescence probes are generally designed. Fluorescence methods involve simple operation and are suitable for real-time detection of analytes. Fluorescent BSA-Au NCs were used for selective DA detection in cerebrospinal fluid (Govindaraju *et al.* 2017). The BSA-Au-NCs showed high fluorescent quantum yield ~ 8%. Quenching of the fluorescence intensity was observed through an electron transfer mechanism after addition of different DA concentrations. Thus, DA was determined in PBS buffer with LOD of 0.622 nM and linear range from 1 to 10 nM. Highly photoluminescent silicon nanoparticles (SiNPs) were synthesized by one-pot microwave-assisted method to detect DA selectively (Zhang *et al.* 2015). Transfer of energy from Si NPs to oxidize DA molecules occurs through FRET. DA molecules quenched the fluorescence of SiNPs, whereas such quenching effect was not observed for other molecules. The LOD obtained was 0.3 nM with a linear range from 0.005 µM to 10.0 µM.

Capillary electrophoresis is a method developed for trace level detection of analytes due to its small sample volume, faster analysis and biocompatibility. High voltages are applied to short capillaries to enable rapid separations. For the detection of neurotransmitters, capillary electrophoresis is generally coupled with mass spectrometry, electrochemical and fluorescence methods. Au/GCNEs were developed to determine cerebral DA (Liu *et al.* 2015). A laser puller was used to pull out size-controlled needle-type quartz capillary. Seed-mediated growth approach was used to chemically functionalize the capillary tip exterior with colloidal gold nanoparticles. The tip was then insulated with cathodic electrophoretic paint followed by heating to produce Au/GCNE with tip apex radius ranging from ~8.9 nm to ~500 nm. The nanoelectrode showed enhanced electrochemical performance with a low LOD of 1.0×10^{-8} M and a wide linear range from 2.0×10^{-8} M to 5.6×10^{-6} M. In yet another work, researchers reported a new sequential injection analysis-capillary electrophoresis system (Fernández et al. 2018). The sequential injection analysis manifold was fully automated and coupled to a capillary electrophoresis apparatus with amperometric detection. A new hydrodynamic injection method was carried out on the basis of overpressure created in the circuit when the pinch valve was closed for a previously determined time. DA was quantified with a linear range from 1 to 500 µM and LOD of 0.3 µM respectively.

2.2 ELECTROCHEMICAL METHOD

Electrochemical method is one of the most preferred technique used for estimation of analyte due to its low cost, ease of fabrication and fast response time. Prior to detailed discussion of DA detection using electrochemical method, a few fundamentals of electrochemical techniques are given below. Several electroanalytical techniques such as voltammetry, coulometry, potentiometry and amperometry are available for precise and specific detection of analytes. A few glimpses on the electrochemical cell configuration are discussed below.

2.2.1 Electrochemical Cell

Figure 2.3 shows the schematic representation of an electrochemical cell which consists of a solution reservoir made of borosilicate glass to store the electrolyte solution covered with a Teflon cap. The electrolyte solution is degassed before the experiments to remove any dissolved oxygen. The concentration of the electrolyte should be almost ten times high compared to the analyte (Lian et al. 2014).

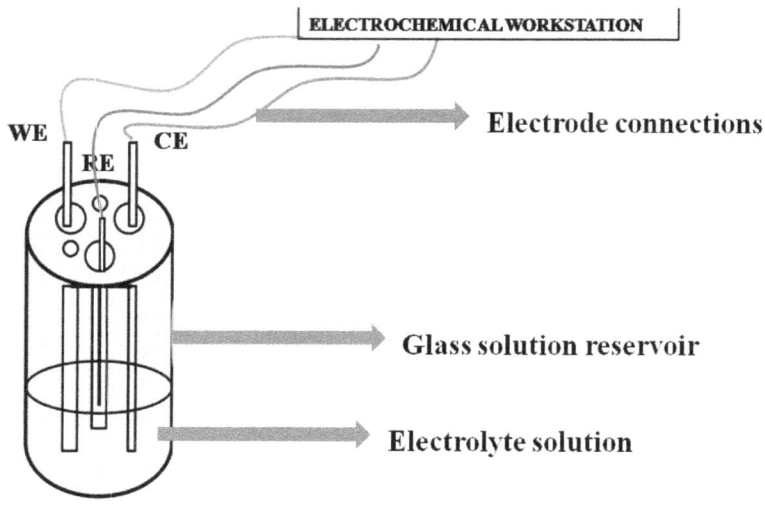

Figure 2.3. Schematic Representation of an Electrochemical Cell

The analysis is usually done in a three electrode configuration viz working electrode, counter electrode and reference electrode respectively.

Working Electrode: All the electrochemical reaction of interest occurs on the working electrode. Several electrodes such as Au, Pt, Ag, glassy carbon, HOPG, carbon paste electrodes etc. serves as the working electrode. The choice of the electrode depends on the desired application and the potential window to be employed. The electrodes should be conducting and stable in acid or alkaline medium. Proper surface pre-treatment is necessary to ensure a clean surface to carry out the measurements.

Counter Electrode- Counter electrode is mostly used to measure the reaction current and it completes the electrical circuit. The surface area of counter electrode should be high compared to that of the working electrode. Mostly Pt wire, Pt mesh and graphite rods are employed in this context.

Reference Electrode- The reaction potential is measured with respect to reference electrode. Some of the commonly used electrodes are SCE with potential 0.2422 V and Ag/AgCl with potential 0.197 V in saturated KCl solution.

2.2.2 Different Electrochemical Techniques

Voltammetry is an electro-analytical technique wherein the current is measured by sweeping a desired potential window. The triangular pulse and the corresponding representation of a cyclic voltammogramm is provided in Figure 2.4.

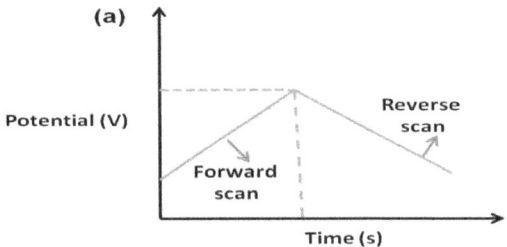

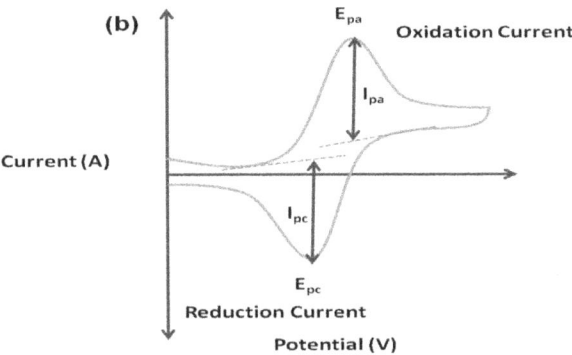

Figure 2.4. (a) Excitation Waveform and (b) Typical Response of CV

In CV a triangular pulse is given as the input and the voltammogramm is recorded from the initial to the final potential. CV is an important technique to infer the redox potentials of the system and also to study the electron transfer kinetics. Most of the redox reactions undergo either a reversible, quasi-reversible or irreversible process (Birke *et al.* 1981). The mass transfer due to the diffusion limited or adsorption limited kinetics can be inferred.

DPV is a sensitive technique employed for the trace level detection of analytes. Herein, a differential pulse of small amplitude was given and the output current will be the difference of forward and the reverse reaction respectively.

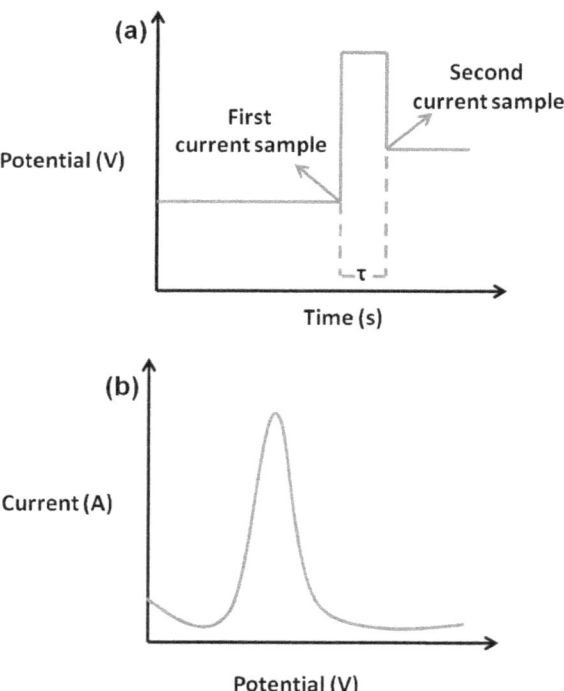

Figure 2.5. (a) Excitation Waveform and (b) Typical Response of DPV

Figure 2.5 shows the differential pulse and the output of a DPV curve. In DPV, the charging current is minimized thereby achieving sharp peak, good sensitivity and low detection limit. The signal to noise ratio is improved by attenuation of the background current.

Chronoamperometry is an electrochemical technique in which the potential of the working electrode is stepped to the region where the reaction occurs and the resulting current from the Faradaic process is monitored as a function of time. It is basically a time-dependent technique wherein the voltage is applied to the cell at V_1 (Figure 2.6) where there is no occurrence of reaction and then it is stepped up to V_2, which initiates the electron transfer process and as a result, there is a spike in the current.

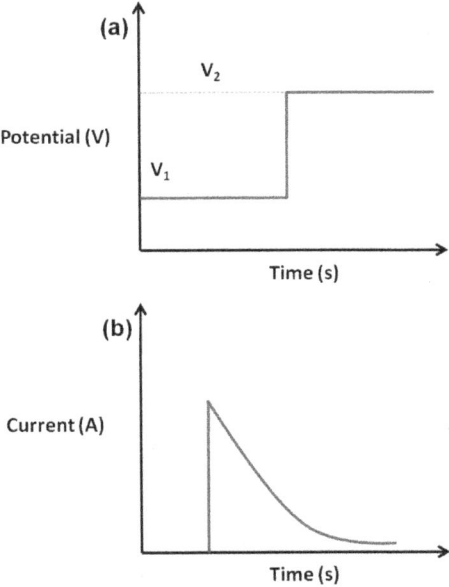

Figure 2.6. (a) Excitation Waveform and (b) Typical Response of Chronoamperometry

Figure 2.6 shows the excitation waveform and the typical response of chronoamperometry. Electrokinetic parameters such as the diffusion coefficient, thickness of the diffusion layer etc. can be estimated from chronoamperometry.

In **EIS,** a small sinusoidal potential or current is applied and the response is measured. The impedance is computed at each frequency. The EIS data is represented either as a vector or complex quantity. The vector is defined by phase angle and impedance magnitude. The complex quantity is given by

$$Z_{total} = Z_{real} + Z_{imag} \tag{2.1}$$

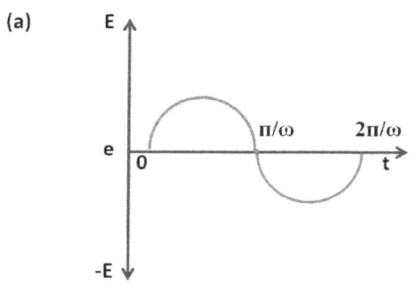

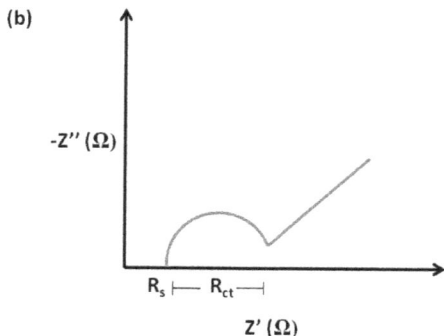

Figure 2.7. (a) Excitation Waveform and (b) Typical Response of EIS

Figure 2.7 shows the excitation waveform and the typical response of EIS. EIS data is displayed as a Nyquist plot (complex plane) or a Bode plot. The processes of individual charge transfer are resolvable in these plots. Modelling of electrochemical cells is done as a network of passive electrical circuit elements where the network is called as an equivalent circuit. The equivalent circuit EIS response can be compared to the actual EIS response of the electrochemical cell.

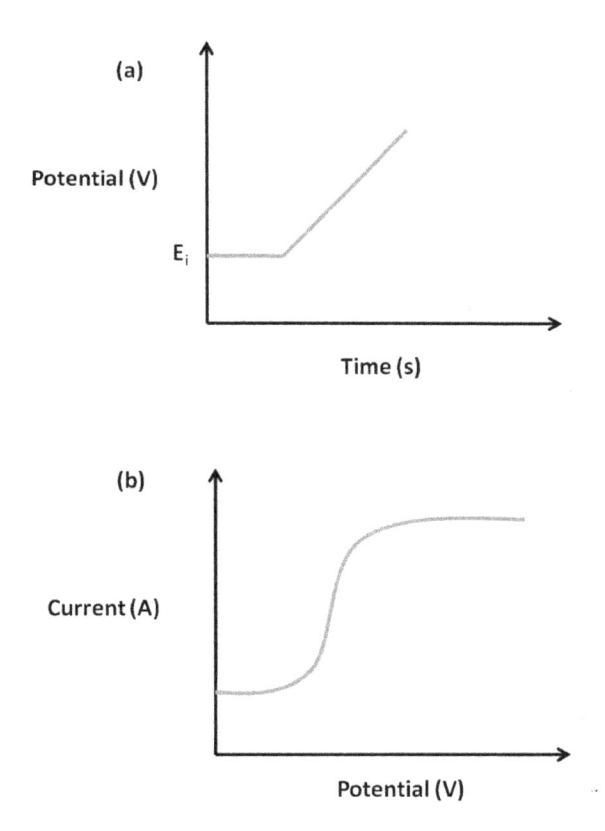

Figure 2.8. (a) Excitation Waveform and (b) Typical Response of Rotating Disk Voltammetry

Figure 2.8 shows the excitation waveform and the typical response of **Rotating disk voltammetry**. Electrode processes at solid surfaces are studied using Rotating disk voltammetry. The RDE consists of a disk usually Glassy carbon or Platinum, which is embedded in a rod of insulating material such as glass, Teflon etc. When the electrode is rotated, mass transfer of reactants and products occur by mechanisms such as convection and diffusion. The convective flow at RDE is similar to the theory of flowing fluids (hydrodynamics) and thus the method is often called as hydrodynamic voltammetry. The centrifugal forces move the liquid horizontally out, creating a hydrodynamic flow pattern.

2.3 ELECTROCHEMICAL METHOD FOR DA DETECTION

As stated above in Section 2.2 in Chapter 2, electrochemical method is a powerful technique that has easy operation, cost effective analysis and fast response time. Generally, it is used to monitor electroactive species like metal ions (cations), anions, biomolecules etc. DA is an electroactive compound and the amount of current required to oxidize DA was used for quantification. Extensive studies have been carried out in the last few decades in this regard.

Though the electrochemical method is an effective technique compared to others, the sensitivity and selectivity are two major issues in DA detection. This is because, the oxidation potentials of Uric Acid (UA) and Ascorbic Acid (AA) are very similar to that of DA and they both act as potential interferents. UA is the end product of purine metabolism and AA is a reducing agent and the concentrations of UA and AA are much higher compared to that of DA (Raj *et al.* 2003). The oxidation products of DA, UA and AA adsorbs on the electrode surface leading to poor reproducibility. The LOD obtained is generally very high, whereas for practical applications, the developed technique and material must detect DA at much lower concentrations. Enormous efforts have been laid by researchers in this aspect to achieve high sensitivity and specificity.

2.3.1 Electrochemistry of DA

The electrochemistry of DA on CMEs was not investigated much until the notable work of Adam *et al.* in 1984 formed the touching stone in studying the redox reaction of DA (Hawley *et al.* 1967, Tse *et al.* 1976). Two ambiguous pathways were proposed for the oxidation of DA, namely the ECE or ECC mechanism. Figure 1.4 depicts the oxidation pathway of DA viz. the initial step is the oxidation of DA to DQH through a $2H^+$, $2e^-$ transfer step followed by deprotonation and intracyclization to form LDC. The LDC either oxidizes to DC (ECE pathway) or combines with DQH to form DA and DC (ECC pathway). The oxidation of DA on pyrolytic graphite electrode was investigated in which it was found that the oxidation occurs through an ECC mechanism (Zhang *et al.* 1993). Similarly, it was reported that the melanization of DA on Carbon Paste Electrode (CPE) proceeds through an ECC mechanism (Young *et al.* and Babbitt *et al.* 1983). Interestingly, a complex ECECEE mechanism for DA at pH above 4 was reported (Li *et al.* 2006). In 2007, the electrochemistry of DA in presence of SDS was studied (Corona-Avendaño *et al.* 2007). An EC mechanism was proposed and the rate constant increases with the increase in SDS concentration. Also in the presence of SDS, the kinetics was transformed from a diffusion controlled to adsorption controlled process. In a similar study, the early oxidation of DA and 5-methyl dopamine was investigated on a carbon electrode (Ismail *et al.* 2016). The authors reported an ECC mechanism which was further supported by quantum chemical calculation. It was stated that, the intracyclization was favoured more in alkaline conditions than in acidic pH.

Apart from GCE, studies on amorphous carbon were also carried out (Palomäki *et al.* 2015). Sluggish electron transfer kinetics was noted on amorphous carbon electrode. The oxidation pathway showed a similar EC mechanism for both Ta-C and GC substrates. Recently, a theoretical approach was employed to investigate the oxidation of DA on an ionic liquid based carbon paste electrode

(Díaz et al. 2013). A change in mechanism from EC to ECE was observed when a Lewis acid group like -CF$_3$ was introduced in the ionic liquid moiety.

2.4 NANOMATERIALS FOR ELECTROCHEMICAL SENSING OF DA

Various metal, metal oxides, core-shell nanostructures, polymers, graphene, carbon based structures etc. based nanomaterials were used in the electrochemical detection of DA.

2.4.1 Metal Nanoparticles

The unique properties of metallic nanoparticles such as high conductivity, high surface area, excellent optical and magnetic properties make them remarkable candidates in diverse fields such as catalysis, drug delivery and energy conversion (Vidhu et al. 2014, Farooq et al. 2018, Liu et al. 2017). Metal nanoparticles like Ag, Au etc. were biosynthesized from Mimosa pudica plant root extract and a sensor was developed to detect DA electrochemically (Sreenivasulu et al. 2016). From the CV response, it was observed that AgNPs-assembled-GCE showed significant increase in peak current compared to bare GCE. The AgNPs/GCE showed a LOD of 0.5 µM and linear range from 10-60 µM. Metal NPs are generally used along with polymers, graphene etc. in the modification of electrodes. Au NPs/OPPy NT arrays were used for development of an electrochemical sensor for DA (Lin et al. 2015). Zinc oxide nanowire arrays were used as templates for electrodeposition of Au NPs/OPPy NT arrays. The electrocatalytic activity of the electrode towards DA was studied using CV and SWV. It was observed that the Au NPs/OPPy NT arrays electrode showed better electrocatalytic activity owing to the increasing electronic conductivity and effective surface area of Au NPs. Simultaneous detection of DA and AA was demonstrated and the electrode showed good selectivity to DA. 2D array of closely packed dendritic platinum nanoparticles decorated free standing graphene paper was developed for ultrasensitive detection of DA secreted by live cells as shown in Figure 2.9. (Zan *et al.* 2016). Oil-water interfacial assembly method was used to maximize the uniform distribution of dendritic NPs on graphene paper. The hybrid electrode showed a LOD of 5 nM and linear range of 87 nM to 100 µM.

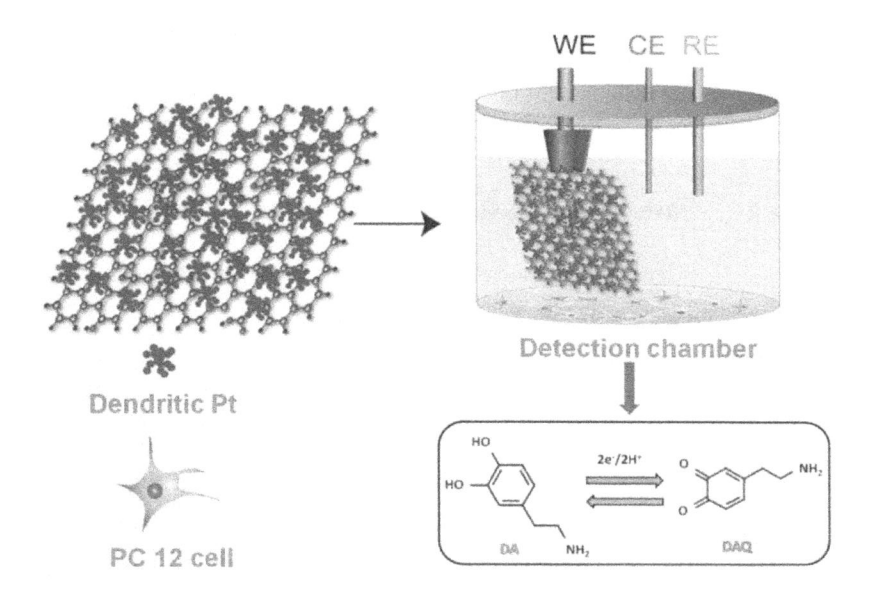

Figure 2.9. Schematic Representation for Electrochemical Detection of DA using Metal Nanoparticles based Composite (Zan *et al.* 2016)

Beta-cyclodextrin can be combined with acid-treated CD-f-PEDOT:PSS to fabricate a highly conductive and electrochemically active film (Qian *et al.* 2018). LOD obtained for DA and catechol in PBS are 9.59 nM and 0.027 µM respectively. The sensor also exhibited good selectivity and reproducibility. Similarly, a nanocomposite comprising of Au NP-graphene (GP) - PEDOT:PSS was used for DA detection (Pananon *et al.* 2018). Selective determination of DA and UA in presence of AA was carried out using AuNP-GP-PEDOT:PSS modified GCE. Peak potential separation between DA and UA was about

110 mV in presence of AA. The AA signal was suppressed significantly and the LOD for DA and UA are 100 pM and 10 µM respectively. And the linear ranges observed for DA and UA are 1 nM to 300 µM and 10 µM to 1 mM respectively. The synergistic effect of AuNP, GP and PEDOT:PSS contributed to greater sensitivity and reduced electrode overpotentials. The electrode also showed excellent stability for about 8 weeks without any major change in the electrochemical response. Further, the recoveries of DA and UA in diluted blood serum ranged from 97.4 % to 106.6% which showed the successful application of the sensor for real sample analysis.

2.4.2 Metal Oxide Nanoparticles

Metal oxide nanoparticles have wide band gap which facilitates the catalytic oxidation of DA, improves the selectivity, stability and sensitivity of the sensor. The most commonly used metal oxides are iron oxide, copper oxide, nickel oxide and cobalt oxide etc. Apart from these, oxide materials of Zn, Al, Mg, Mn, Sn, Zr were also employed. An electrochemical sensor based on flower shaped ZnO nanoparticles was shown to detect DA with high selectivity (Balram *et al.* 2018). Low oxidation potential and high oxidation peak current was observed for ZnO modified GCE compared to bare GCE. LOD for DA was 0.04 µM and the linear range was 0.1 to 16 µM. The sensor also showed good selectivity to various interferents such as glucose, catechol, UA, AA etc. MoO_x NPs were synthesized by pulsed laser ablation technique in water (Fazio *et al.* 2018). Then, SPCE was modified with the synthesized MoO_x NPs. Detection of DA was carried out in PBS at pH 7. The linear concentration for DA was in the range of 0.1 µM to 600 µM with a LOD of 43 nM.

It is well known that, the performance of the sensor depends on the size and shape of the nanomaterials. For instance, copper (I) oxide nanospheres supported graphene was reported (Mei *et al.* 2016). The porous nanospheres were obtained by a solvothermal method with hexadecyl trimethyl ammonium bromide as the capping agent. The sensor showed a LOD of 15 nM for DA and linear range from 0.05 µM to 109 µM. The incorporation of porosity in the nanostructure showed an improvement in the detection limit. Magnetic nanoparticles like cobalt oxide and iron oxide has also been investigated for the detection of dopamine. In yet another work, the performance of N-doped graphene-cobalt oxide nanocomposite was evaluated towards detection of DA (Yasmin et al. 2016). Doping of heteroatoms like N to the graphene sheets improves the conductivity and provides more active sites for catalysis. In the reported work, the nanocomposite was prepared by a hydrothermal method.

The investigation yielded a low detection limit of 0.029 µM, linear range from 0.3 µM -800.8 µM and a high sensitivity of 369 µA µM^{-1}cm^{-2}. The significance of this sensor is the unhindered detection of DA in the presence of excess concentration of AA.

Hybrid composites consisting of PPy coated on Fe$_3$O$_4$-rGO showed excellent response towards DA with good sensitivity. The Fe$_3$O$_4$-rGO was prepared by a solvothermal method over which the PTSA doped PPy was coated through wet chemical synthesis (Wang et al. 2016). The PTSA doping improved the conductivity and thereby the overall performance of the electrode. The detection limit and linear range was reported as 2.3 nM and 70 nM – 20 µM. In addition to the above, Table 2.1 summarizes the performance of different metal oxide modified electrodes in DA sensing.

Table 2.1. Performance of Metal Oxides Modified Electrodes in DA Sensing

Electrode	Method	Limit of Detection (LOD) µM	Linear Range µM	Sensitivity µA µM^{-1} cm^{-2}	Ref
Fe$_3$O$_4$-Co$_3$O$_4$/rGO	CA	0.13	0.5-1550	0.26	(Han et al. 2016)
MoO$_x$/SPCE	SWV	0.043	0.01-650	-	(Chen et al. 2018)
r-GO-SnO$_2$/GCE	DPV	0.006	0.08-30	-	(Ma et al. 2015)

Table 2.1 (Continued)

Electrode	Method	Limit of Detection (LOD) µM	Linear Range µM	Sensitivity µA µM^{-1} cm^{-2}	Ref
Flower shaped ZnO	DPV	0.04	0.1-16	4.38	(Balram et al. 2018)
GNP/FTO	DPV	0.22	30-100	0.15	(Rahman et al. 2017)
γ-WO$_3$/GCE	DPV	0.024	0.1-50, 50-600	-	(Anithaa et al. 2015)
OFMs-modified GCE	CA	0.03	0.2-115	1.01	(Chen et al. 2018)
ZnO NWAs/GF	DPV	0.05	0.05-20	3.15	(Yue et al. 2017)
MoO$_x$/SPCE	SWV	0.043	0.01-650	-	(Fazio et al. 2018)
IL-TiO$_2$/GO/GCE	DPV	0.0009	0.008-60	-	(Lv et al. 2016)
MnO$_2$NWs-ErGO/GCE	SDLSV	0.001	0.06-1.0, 1.0-80	-	(He et al. 2018)
CeO$_2$-HEG-nafion@GCE	CA	1	10-780	-	(Nayak et al. 2015)
CS-Nd$_{ox}$/GCE	SWV	0.079	-	-	(Nagles et al. 2017)
Tyrosinase/NiO/ITO	CV	1.04	2-100	0.06	(Roychoudhury et al. 2016)

rGO-reduced graphene oxide, SPCE- screen printed carbon electrode, GCE- glassy carbon electrode, GNP- graphene nanoplatelet, FTO- fluorine-doped tin oxide, OFM- olive-like Fe$_2$O$_3$ microspheres, NWAs- nanowire arrays, GF- graphene foam, ErGO-electrochemically reduced graphene oxide, IL-ionic liquid, NWs- nanowires, HEG-Hydrogen exfoliated graphene, CS-chitosan, ITO-Indium tin oxide

2.4.3 Core-shell Nanostructures

Core-shell nanostructures are excellent candidates for electrochemical biosensors due to its preferential structural arrangement of core and shell. The properties can be tailored during the synthesis process. For instance the synthesis of monodispersed Au@CdS hybrid core-shell structure was carried out by a self-assemble method (Zhang et al. 2015). The Au@CdS hybrid core-shell NPs are negatively charged and attracts the positively charged DA cation by electrostatic interaction. The biosensor showed a wide linear range from 0.002 to 800 µM with a LOD of 0.55 nM. The biosensor was used for real-time quantitative analysis of DA for biological applications. To simultaneously detect AA, DA and UA, rGO-bimetallic Pd@Au nanocomposites were fabricated (Zou *et al.* 2016). The Pd core and Au shell nanostructures were found to be distributed homogeneously on the rGO surface. The GCE modified with (Pd@Au)/rGO showed excellent electron transfer, selectivity and sensitivity for DA detection. Three distinct peaks were observed for AA, DA and UA. The LOD and linear ranges are as follows DA-0.2 µM and 1 to 400.56 µM; AA-24.88 µM and 50 to 2856.63 µM and UA-1.25 µM and 5 to 680.76 µM.

Pt/CeO$_2$@Cu$_2$O nanocomposite based electrode was used for detection of DA and PA as shown in Figure 2.10 (Rajamani *et al.* 2018).

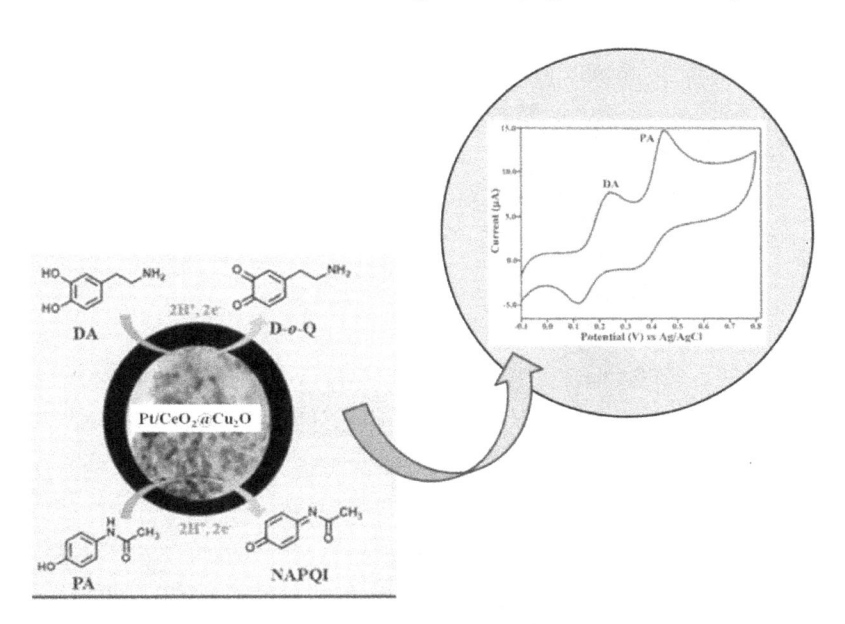

Figure 2.10. Schematic Representation for Electrochemical Detection of DA and PA using Core-shell Nanostructure (Rajamani *et al.* 2018)

The nanocomposite was synthesized by low temperature galvanic replacement method involving phase interfacial reaction. Strong core shell formation was observed due to the interfacial involvement between Cu_2O and CeO_2. $Pt/CeO_2@Cu_2O$ carbon based electrode exhibited high electrocatalytic activity for individual and simultaneous detection of DA and PA. The oxidation peak potentials for DA and PA was observed at 160 mV and 380 mV respectively. The linear concentration range obtained for both DA and PA was 0.5 µM to 100 µM and the corresponding LOD values are 0.079 µM and 0.091 µM.

Further an electrochemical sensor was designed based on $GO/Fe_3O_4@SiO_2$ core shell nanocomposite modified SPE for determination of DA and UA (Beitollahi *et al.* 2017). The LOD and linear range are as follows: for DA 8.9×10^{-8} M and 0.1 to 600 µM; for UA 5.7×10^{-7} µM and 0.75 to 300 µM. The SPEs were also successfully employed for measurement of DA and UA in dopamine injection and urine samples. Nanoflowers of Au@Pt supported on graphene oxide (Au@Pt/GO) were reported for electrochemical sensing of DA (Yang *et al.* 2018). The nanocomposite was synthesized by a wet-chemical co-reduction method. A very low LOD of 0.11 µM and linear range from 0.5 µM to 0.1775 mM was observed for DA.

2.4.4 CNT based nanocomposite

CNTs have a large surface-to-volume ratio (~2500 m^2g^{-1}) and hence promote rapid electron transfer reactions. CNT modified electrodes are widely used in the detection of bioanalytes because of their increased selectivity and sensitivity as shown in Figure 2.11 (Wang *et al.* 2018). CNTs are attractive materials for making smaller electrodes with good biocompatibility. A highly selective DA sensor was fabricated by synthesizing electrospun PA6/PAH nanofibers and functionalizing them with MWCNT (Mercante *et al.* 2015). PA6 and PAH was sufficiently mixed together to form nanofibers onto which the MWCNTs were attached strongly. The functionalized nanofibers were coated on ITO electrodes. The electrode showed a LOD of 0.15 µM and a linear response from 1 to 70 µM for DA. Microelectrodes can be modified with CNTs for detection of neurotransmitters (Yang et al. 2016). CNTs were grown on metal wires and investigated as microelectrodes for determination of DA. The bare CFMEs were compared with CNT-Nb microelectrodes. From the results, the CNT-Nb microelectrodes showed higher sensitivity and lower ΔE_p value compared to CNTs grown on metal wires and carbon fibers. Two fold lower LOD about 11 ± 1 nM was observed for CNT-Nb microelectrodes than bare CFMEs. The CNT-Nb microelectrodes were also used for monitoring stimulated release of DA in anesthetized rats.

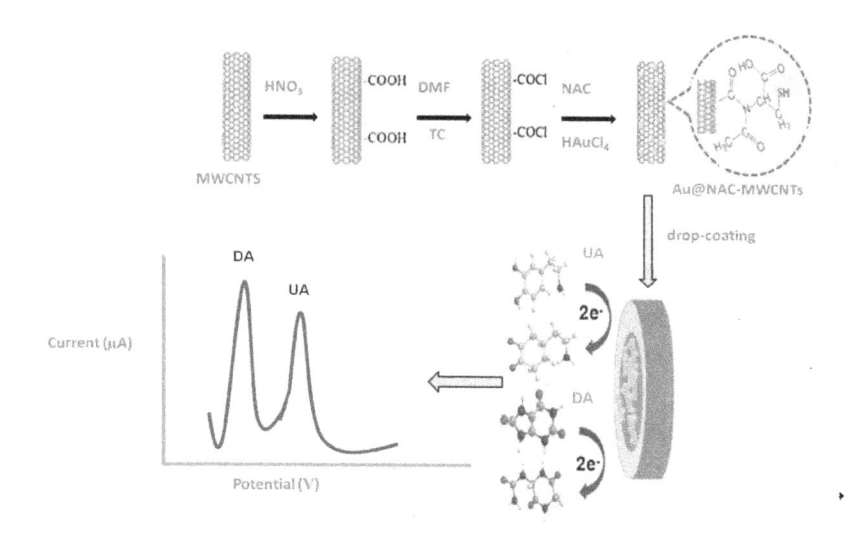

Figure 2.11. Electrochemical Detection of DA using CNT based Nanocomposite (Wang et al. 2018)

Phthalocyanine doped metal oxide nanoparticles (Fe_3O_4, ZnO) and functionalized MWCNTs hybrids were modified on GCE (MO/Pc/MWCNT) for electrochemical detection of DA (Mphuthi et al. 2017). The best electrocatalytic activity towards DA oxidation was achieved by the electrode GCE-MWCNT/ ZnO/29H, 31H-Pc with very low LOD of 0.75 µM. The DA oxidation was diffusion controlled but adsorption of some reaction intermediate products was also characterized. The electrocatalytic property was attributed to the frontier molecular orbital energy levels and electronegativities. 29H, 31H-Pc showed better performance because of its good electron accepting ability. In a particular work, hybrid material consisting of molybdenum sulphide flowers placed on graphene nanosheets and MWCNTs (GNS-CNTs/MoS$_2$) was synthesized (Mani *et al.* 2016). The composite was shown to have high capacitance current, large electrochemically active surface area, high conductivity, large porosity and wide potential window. The sensor showed a low LOD of 50 nM and the DA concentration was linear in the range of 100 nM to 100 µM. The sensor was also applied to DA determination in biological and pharmaceutical samples.

2.4.5 Mixed Metal Oxides

MMO nanoparticles generally consist of two metals (mostly transition elements) in the matrix and thus they possess unique electronic and magnetic properties. MMOs are commonly used in the field of catalysis, solar cells, supercapacitors etc.

2.4.5.1 Spinels

Spinels have a general formula of AB$_2$X$_4$ as shown in Figure 2.12 where A and B are metal cations and X is the anion (mostly oxygen). Spinels exhibit ferromagnetic properties, high catalytic activity and are thus used in applications such as catalysis, sensing, biomedicine, lithium ion batteries etc. (Goyal *et al.* 2017, Zhao *et al.* 2013, Yue *et al.* 2018).

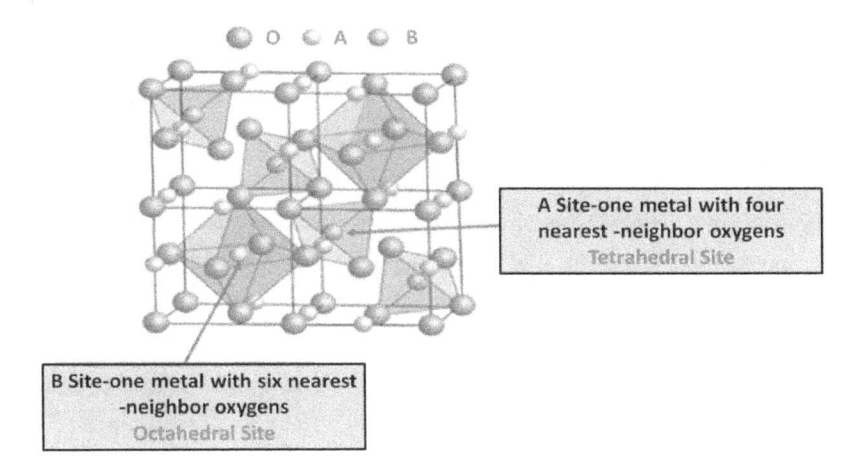

Figure 2.12. Structure of AB$_2$X$_4$ Spinel

A sensitive electrochemical sensor for DA detection was developed based on OM- ZnFe$_2$O$_4$ (Huang *et al.* 2020). The OM- ZnFe$_2$O$_4$ was prepared by a facile nanocasting method. The OM- ZnFe$_2$O$_4$ modified electrode showed excellent activity for oxidation of DA with a sensitivity of 0.094 nA nM^{-1}. A very low detection limit of 0.4 nM with a wide linear range from 2 to 600 nM was observed. The modified electrode was further used to monitor the increase in DA concentration induced by K$^+$ - stimulation of living PC12 cells in neurological environment. Similarly, nanocomposite of CuAl$_2$O$_4$/CuO was synthesized and applied for electrochemical detection of DA (Zaidan *et al.* 2019). The nanocomposite was prepared by sol-gel method using NaB(C$_6$H$_5$)$_4$ as the capping agent. From DPV, the LOD for DA was found to be 0.08 μM and the linear ranges were 0.5 to 1 μM and 1 to 20 μM. The sensor also showed good anti-interference property. A soft-template (citrate)-assisted method followed by calcination was used for the synthesis of novel spinel-type CCO NPs (Balasubramanian *et al.* 2019). The metal cations such as Cu^{2+} and Co^{2+} reacts with the citrate molecules by means of coordination interaction to form CuCo – citrate at high temperatures. Then, calcinations was done at 400 °C to eliminate the citrate molecules leading to successful formation of CCO NPs. The CCO NPs based sensor was employed for the detection of ACh. The sensor showed a LOD of 30 nM and a linear range from 0.2 to 3500 µM. The point-of-care use of the sensor was demonstrated in spiked blood serum samples with acceptable recovery rates. In addition, other spinel based structures such as $ZnCo_2O_4$, $MnCo_2O_4$, $NiCo_2O_4$ as shown in Figure 2.13 were also employed for the detection of DA (Naik *et al.* 2015, Kaur *et al.* 2015).

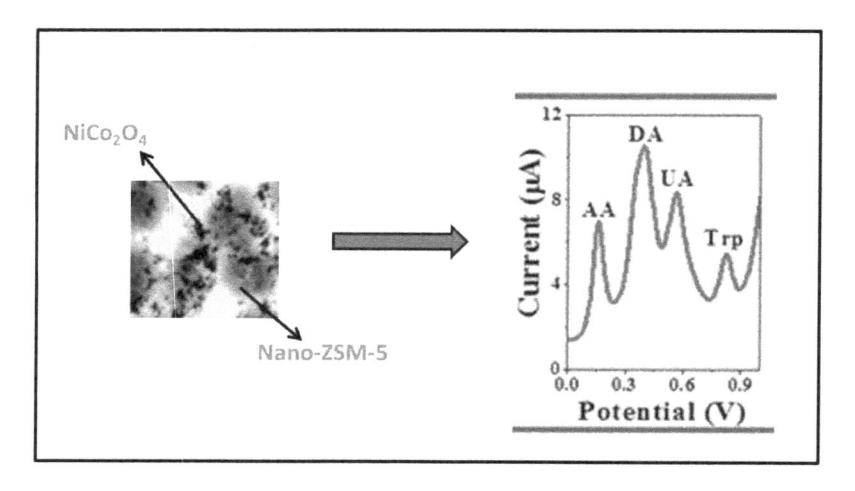

Figure 2.13. Spinel Structure for Electrochemical Detection of DA (Kaur *et al.* 2015)

2.4.5.2 Perovskites

Perovskites are large family of oxide compounds with ABO_3 crystal structure as shown in Figure 2.14 where A and B are metal cations and O is an oxygen anion. The A cation occupies the 12-fold co-ordination site which is formed in the middle of the cube of corner sharing BO_6 octahedra. Perovskites are mostly cubic in structure; however phase transitions can be achieved at lower temperatures.

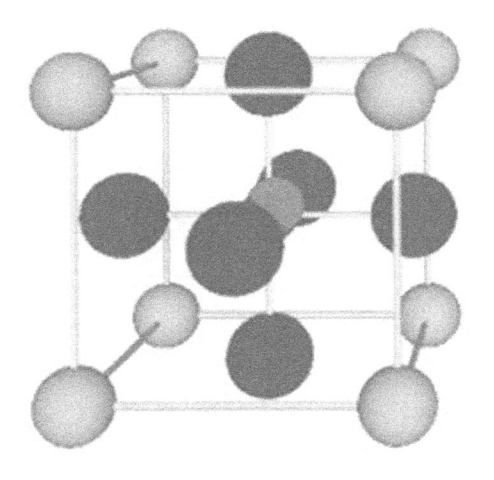

Figure 2.14. Structure of ABO₃ Perovskite

Perovskites are fascinating materials to be studied since they can exhibit a variety of properties such as thermoelectric, magnetic, high electronic conductivity, thermal and chemical stability etc. Moreover, perovskites has an active structure in which the oxide ions can move within the crystal leading to oxygen deficiencies. Also, it is flexible to vary the composition of metal ions since the structure can incorporate ions that have different size and charge. The electronic properties of the perovskites can thus be altered by substituting ions in the A-site or B-site or deviating from the ideal stoichiometry. Almost, 90% of the elements present in the periodic table are stable in the perovskite structure. There are two major requirements for the formation of perovskite structure namely i) electroneutrality-the charge distribution must be appropriate and ii) r_A must be larger than 0.090 nm; the r_B must be larger than 0.051 nm and t must have values in the range of $0.8 < t < 1.0$.

Perovskites are used as electrode modifiers and exhibit much higher activity than metal oxides. The high catalytic activity of perovskites is partially associated with high surface activity, oxygen deficient sites and presence of two or more transition elements. Perovskites are employed as catalysts in oxygen reduction and hydrogen evolution reactions (Jung *et al.* 2014, Xu *et al.* 2016). They are also used in fuel cells especially in SOFC as effective anodic catalysts (Huang *et al.* 2006). For photovoltaic solar cell applications, perovskites exhibit very good stability and high efficiency. Some of the recent applications of perovskites are electrochemical sensing of glucose, H_2O_2, gases, alcohols and neurotransmitters (Jia *et al.* 2015, Zhang *et al.* 2012, Atta *et al.* 2014). The catalytic performance is increased in terms of selectivity, stability, sensitivity, anti-interference ability and reproducibility.

Some of the perovskite oxides that are widely used for gas sensing applications are $LaFeO_3$ and $SrTiO_3$. They are highly suitable for gas sensing due to their ideal band gap (3-4eV), thermal stability, catalytic property etc. Perovskite based biosensors were also developed for detection of H_2O_2 and glucose. The sensors showed good biocompatibility and also very low detection limits were achieved. Perovskites such as $LaFeO_3$ (Figure 2.15) and $SrPdO_3$ were employed for the detection of DA.

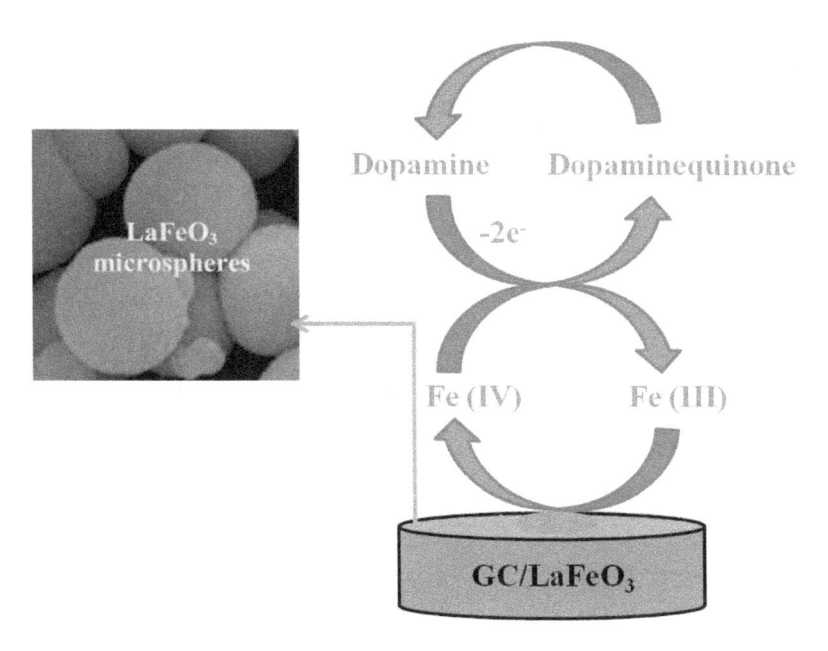

Figure 2.15. Schematic Representation for Electrochemical Detection of DA using Perovskite Nanostructure (Thirumalairajan *et al.* 2014)

Oxygen-surface interaction between oxygen atoms of the hydroxyl groups and the transition elements in the perovskite was shown to be responsible for the increase in catalytic activity. Perovskite is known for its oxygen deficient sites and thus the dihydroxy oxygen adsorbs onto these sites by forming a moderate bond between oxygen atoms and transition elements. Table 2.2 shows the perovskite based sensors for detection of H_2O_2, glucose and DA.

Table 2.2. Performance of Perovskites in the Electrochemical Detection of H_2O_2, Glucose and DA

Perovskite	Analyte	Limit of detection (LOD) µM	Sensitivity µA mM^{-1} cm^{-2}	Ref
LaTiO$_3$-Ag0.1	glucose	0.0025	780	(Jia et al. 2015)
LaNi$_{0.6}$Co$_{0.4}$O$_3$	H_2O_2 and glucose	0.001 H_2O_2, 0.008 glucose	1812.84 H_2O_2, 643.0 glucose	(Zhang et al. 2012)
Co$_{0.4}$Fe$_{0.6}$LaO$_3$	H_2O_2 and glucose	0.002 H_2O_2, 0.01 glucose	-	(Zhang et al. 2013)
Graphite/SrPdO$_3$/ Au$_{nano}$	glucose	10.1	422.30	(Ekram et al. 2015)
LaNiO$_3$	H_2O_2 and glucose	0.033	-	(Wang et al. 2013)
LaFeO$_3$ microspheres	DA	0.059	-	(Thirumalairajan et al. 2014)
CpE/SrPdO$_3$	DA	0.0093	-	(Atta et al. 2014)
LaFeO$_3$ nanoparticles	DA	0.03	-	(Wang et al. 2009)
Graphite/SrPdO$_3$	DA	0.0016	-	(Atta et al. 2013)
LaCoO$_3$	DA	3.53	-	(Priyatharshni et al. 2017)

CpE-carbon paste electrode

2.5 CHALLENGES IN DA DETECTION AND MOTIVATION OF THE WORK

Although perovskite based sensors were reported for DA detection, till date the material has not been much explored for sensing application. Moreover the detection limit, sensitivity and selectivity of the sensor need to be improved to match the level of DA in human body. Another challenge is to improve the stability of the sensor, an important parameter to decide its long term employability in the field. Attempts have been made to address the above mentioned problems in this thesis. Fe and Ti based pervoskite (FeTiO$_3$) was chosen for this purpose. Both Fe and Ti are conductive and possess good catalytic properties. In addition the oxygen deficient sites enhance the sensing ability of the sensor. The FeTiO$_3$ based nanostructures were employed for the sensing of DA and studies were carried out to understand the mechanistic pathway of DA oxidation on FeTiO$_3$. Also a polymer capping was introduced in the nanostructure to improve the stability of the sensor.

2.6 SUMMARY

The review briefly described the different techniques that are available for detection of DA such as colorimetry, ECL, HPLC, fluorescence, capillary electrophoresis etc. The advantages of electrochemical method over other methods were highlighted. Fundamentals of electrochemical experiments and the electrochemical experiments such as CV, DPV, Chronoamperometry, EIS and Rotating Disk Voltammetry were also discussed. Electrochemical method for DA detection was explained briefly wherein literatures on the electrochemistry of DA on CMEs and studies on the oxidation pathway of DA was pointed out. Different nanomaterials such as metals, metal oxides, core-shell nanostructures, polymers, graphene etc. used in electrochemical detection of DA to improve the selectivity and sensitivity of detection was mentioned. Significance of mixed metal oxide based nanostructures such as spinels and perovskites was also discussed elaborately.

From the review, it is inferred that enhanced performance could be achieved by modification of the electrode surface with suitable nanostructures. Sensitivity of detection can be enhanced by improving electron transfer at the electrode surface. The electrocatalytic activity for DA detection after chemical modification of the electrode surface with functional groups or ions improves the selectivity in presence of interferents such as UA and AA. Simultaneous detection of DA, UA and AA was also achieved. In order to face the current challenges in DA detection, it is important to develop stable, cost-effective material for electrode modification. Synthesis of modification materials, electrodes with better kinetics, long term stability and reproducibility are important for production of commercial sensors to be used in real time applications.

CHAPTER 3

FeTiO$_3$ NANOHEXAGONS BASED ELECTROCHEMICAL SENSOR FOR THE DETECTION OF DOPAMINE

3.1 INTRODUCTION

As mentioned in chapter 2, Perovskite is one of the emerging nanomaterials having excellent physical and chemical properties with extensive applications in the field of SOFC, batteries etc. (Tao *et al*. 2003 and Hardin *et al*. 2013). The presence of oxygen deficient sites imparts unique properties to perovskites. Although, perovskites have been vastly studied, only recently they were employed as effective materials for sensor application (Atta *et al*. 2014). LaFeO$_3$ microspheres and LaMnO$_3$ nanospheres were reported by Ponpandian *et al.* for the electrochemical determination of DA (Thirumalairajan *et al*. 2012 and Priyatharshni *et al*. 2016). Among the various perovskites, FeTiO$_3$ (Ilmenite) is a natural mineral commonly found as an inclusion in kimberlites (García-Muñoz *et al*. 2016). FeTiO$_3$ is a semiconductor with a wide bandgap in the range of 2.58 eV to 2.90 eV (Truong *et al*. 2012, Kim *et al*. 2009 and Ribeiro *et al*. 2015). The presence of multiple oxidation states in the FeTiO$_3$ and the generation of oxygen vacancies lead to enhanced catalytic activity (Johnsson *et al*. 2008, Hernandez *et al*. 2002, Modeshia *et al*. 2010, Joshi *et al*. 2008, Mao *et al*. 2003, Niderberger *et al*. 2004 and Guan *et al*. 2013). Although FeTiO$_3$ has been studied for various applications their performance towards the detection of DA has not been explored much.

The present chapter deals with the development of an electrochemical biosensor based on FeTiO$_3$ nanostructures for detection of DA in presence of the interfering agents. The nanostructure was prepared by a simple hydrothermal method using urea as the structure directing agent, eliminating high temperature calcination. The FeTiO$_3$ modified electrode was employed for the detection of DA and the validity of the sensor was tested in human biological fluids.

3.2   MATERIALS AND METHODS

3.2.1   Chemicals

Fe$_2$SO$_4$.7H$_2$O (Merck, ≥99%), urea (Merck, ≥99%), titanium isopropoxide (Sisco Chemicals), ethanol (≥99.5%, Merck), dopamine hydrochloride (≥98%, Himedia), UA (≥99%, Himedia), K$_2$HPO$_4$ (≥98%, Merck), KH$_2$PO$_4$ (≥98%, Merck), KOH (≥85%, Merck), KNO$_3$ (Merck, ≥99%), KCl (Merck≥99.5%), and glucose (Merck ≥99.5%) were used as procured. The solutions needed for the experiments were prepared using Millipore water with a resistivity of 18 MΩ cm.

3.2.2   Synthesis of FeTiO$_3$ nanohexagons

A simple protocol was carried out for the synthesis of FeTiO$_3$ nanostructures (Guan *et al.* 2013). About 1.2 mL of titanium isopropoxide was added to a premixed solution of 10 % urea and 20 mL of deionized water. The solution was then stirred well for 30 minutes. To the above mixture 1.112 g of FeSO$_4$.7H$_2$O was added which resulted in the formation of a brown suspension. The pH of the Solution was then adjusted to 14 using 1 M KOH solution. After stirring for a minute, the solution was transferred to a Teflon lined autoclave and the hydrothermal reaction was carried out at 200 °C for 10 h. The resulting dark brown precipitate was centrifuged, washed with deionized water and ethanol several times and dried at 80 °C.

3.2.3 Material Characterization

The material was characterized by TEM using JEOL JEM 2100, Japan equipped with EDX analysis. The determination of crystal structure was carried out from the XRD patterns obtained from Bruker D8 Advance (Japan) equipped with Cu Kα radiation source with λ of 1.54 Å. The chemical structure was confirmed using FTIR Schimadzu IR Affinity 1S (Japan). The elemental analysis was performed using XPS from PHI 5000 Versa II, FEI Inc. The deconvolution of the XPS spectrum was performed using XPS peak fit software. The surface area of the material was measured from BET analysis using Quant Chrome Autosorb 1C analyzer.

3.2.4 Electrochemical Measurements

All the electrochemical experiments were performed in a three electrode cell assembly comprising of a GCE with 3 mm diameter (0.07 cm^2) as the working electrode, platinum wire as the counter electrode and an Ag/AgCl in 3 M KCl as the reference electrode. The initial step in the preparation of the working electrode involves cleaning of the electrode surface with alumina paste followed by repeated washing with water and ethanol under sonication for 5 minutes. The as cleaned working electrode was then modified with the suspension prepared by dissolving 1 mg of the FeTiO$_3$ in 1 mL of ethanol. The suspension was ultrasonicated for about 15 minutes to get a uniform distribution. About 10 μL of the suspension was dropcasted on the electrode surface followed by drying. Electrochemical experiments such as CV, DPV, CA and EIS was carried out with the three electrode assembly setup in a Biologic Instrument, Multichannel VSP Potentiostat/Galvanostat, France. The CV analysis was performed on bare GCE and FeTiO$_3$/GCE from a solution of 0.1 mM DA in 0.1 M PBS solution between the potential range of 0 V to 0.8 V at a scan rate of 100 mV/s. Similarly, the selective detection of DA was studied using DPV from a solution of 0.1 M PBS in a potential range of - 0.2 V and

0.5 V. 5 mM stock solution of DA and UA were used for the electrochemical studies. EIS was performed to analyse the electrochemical kinetics of the FeTiO$_3$/GCE in 0.1 M PBS and 5 mM K$_4$[Fe(CN)$_6$] at their OCV in the frequency range of 10^6 Hz to 0.01 Hz.

3.2.5 Analysis of Real Samples

The validity of the proposed method was evaluated with diluted serum and urine samples. Around 100 μL of the serum and urine samples was diluted in 0.1 M PBS solution. Different concentrations of DA and UA were added using the standard addition method and the DPV analysis was carried out. The amount of DA and UA was estimated by comparing the obtained peak current with the calibration graph.

3.3 RESULTS AND DISCUSSION

3.3.1 Characterization of FeTiO$_3$

3.3.1.1 Morphological characterization of FeTiO$_3$

Figure 3.1 shows the TEM image of FeTiO$_3$ prepared through the hydrothermal method. Nanohexagons with a diameter of around 300 nm were observed in the TEM image (Figure 3.1). Figure 3.1a shows the wide distribution of FeTiO$_3$ nanohexagons. Figure 3.1 (b and c) shows the FeTiO$_3$ nanohexagons at a magnification of 200 nm. The structure seems to be perfect hexagonal with an angle of ~120°. The electron diffraction pattern indicates the crystalline nature of FeTiO$_3$ and the interplanar spacing showed the presence of (001) plane from the spot pattern (Figure 3.1d). Figure 3.1e shows the EDX image indicating the presence of Fe, Ti and O elements.

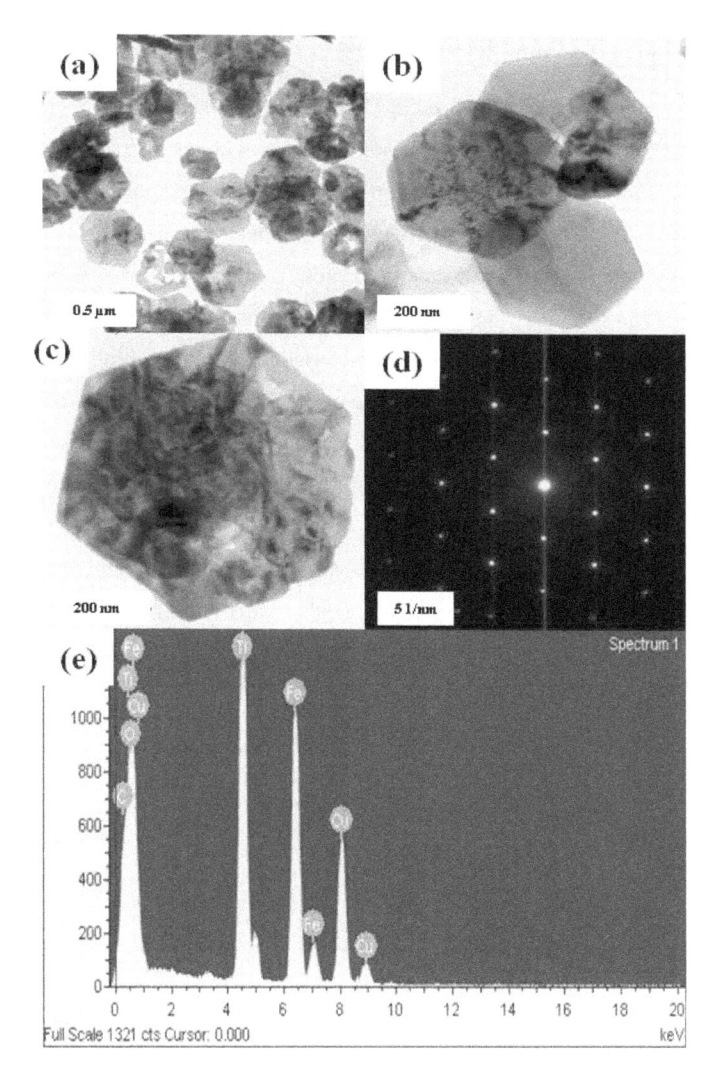

Figure 3.1. (a-c) TEM Images of FeTiO$_3$ Recorded at Different Magnifications; (d) the Corresponding SAED Pattern and (e) shows the EDX Image Respectively

3.3.1.2 XRD and FTIR Analysis

FeTiO$_3$ nanostructure was characterized using XRD and FTIR. Figure 3.2a shows the XRD pattern of FeTiO$_3$ with the diffraction peaks at 23.8°, 32.7°, 35.4°, 40.5°, 49.1°, 53.4°, 62.0° and 63.9° corresponding to (012), (104), (110), (113), (024), (116), (214) and (300) planes respectively. The diffraction peaks were indexed to the ilmenite structure with respect to JCPDS reference no. 29-0733. Similarly, the FTIR spectrum shows the presence of a broad peak at around 3427 cm^{-1}, which is a characteristic stretching vibration of -OH group. A small peak at 2976 cm^{-1} was due to the stretching vibrations of C–H and the peaks observed at 1527 cm^{-1} and 1361 cm^{-1} are attributed to asymmetrical and symmetrical stretching vibration of O–C=O respectively. The C–O stretching vibration of C–OH was observed at 1112 cm^{-1}. The peaks at 600 cm^{-1} and 547 cm^{-1} correspond to the Ti-O stretching vibration and Fe-O stretching vibration respectively (Figure 3.2b) (Palanisamy *et al.* 2019).

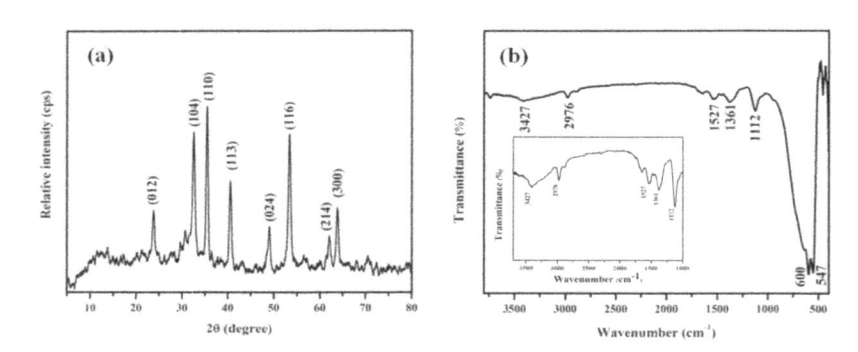

Figure 3.2. (a) XRD Pattern and (b) FTIR Spectrum of FeTiO$_3$ Nanostructure and the Inset Shows the Expanded View in the Region between 3500 cm^{-1} to 1000 cm^{-1}

3.3.1.3 XPS analysis of FeTiO₃

The XPS survey spectrum in Figure 3.3a shows the presence of elements Fe, Ti, O and a small amount of adventitious carbon on the surface. Figure 3.3b depicts the deconvoluted spectrum of Fe 2p, in which two dominated peaks for Fe $2p_{3/2}$ and Fe $2p_{1/2}$ was observed at 710.44 eV and 723.51 eV respectively. At 714.9 eV, a satellite peak is present in between the Fe $2p_{3/2}$ and Fe $2p_{1/2}$ peaks. In addition, peaks at 730.92 eV and 710.08 eV were also noticed. From the results, it is confirmed that the XPS peaks of Fe correspond to Fe^{3+} and Fe^{2+} oxidation states.

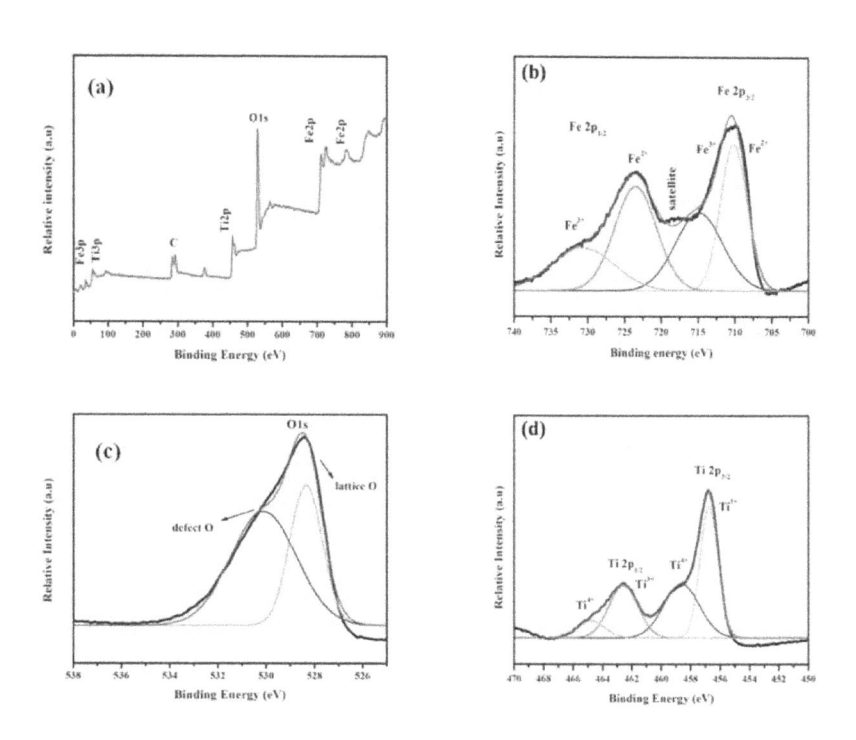

Figure 3.3. XPS Spectrum of FeTiO₃ (a) Survey Spectrum, (b) Fe 2p, (c) O 1s and (d) Ti 2p Respectively

The O1s peak is shown in Figure 3.3c, with a strong peak at 528.33 eV, which corresponds to the characteristic signal lattices of O in the FeTiO₃ and a shoulder peak at 530.10 eV is assigned to the defect O components i.e. oxygen vacancies and adsorbed oxygen on the lattices (Guo *et al.* 2016). Figure 3.3d shows the Ti 2p deconvoluted spectrum, where peaks at 464.70 eV and 462.55 eV were observed, which could be attributed to Ti $2p_{1/2}$ and peaks at 458.62 eV and 456.78 eV are assigned to Ti $2p_{3/2}$. From Figure 3.3 d it is seen that Ti also exists as Ti^{3+}/Ti^{4+} oxidation states in the material.

3.3.1.4   Nitrogen Adsorption/Desorption Studies of FeTiO$_3$

In order to deduce the surface area of the FeTiO$_3$ nanostructures the nitrogen adsorption/desorption (BET) studies were carried out as shown in Figure 3.4. The study revealed that the FeTiO$_3$ nanostructures belong to Type II isotherms with a surface area of 139.5 $m^2 g^{-1}$ and the average pore diameter of 7.8 nm. The pore volume was calculated to be 0.648 $cm^3 g^{-1}$. The obtained surface area was found to be high compared to other FeTiO$_3$ nanoparticles reported in literature (Guan *et al.* 2013). The presence of high surface area can contribute to improved catalytic activity of FeTiO$_3$.

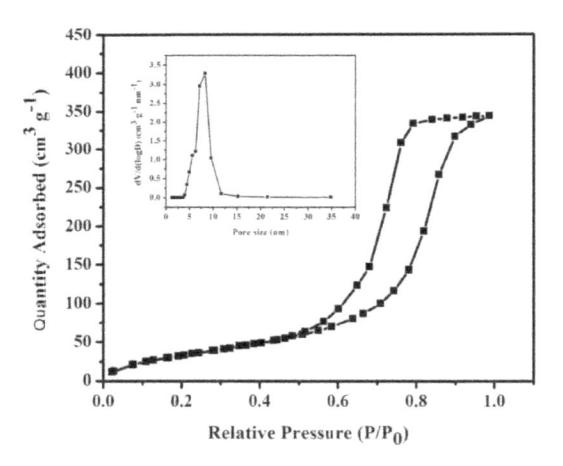

Figure 3.4. Nitrogen Adsorption/Desorption Isotherm Curves of FeTiO$_3$ Nanostructures and the Inset Depicts the Pore Size Distribution

3.3.1.5 EIS spectrum of FeTiO$_3$

The FeTiO$_3$/GCE was electrochemically characterized in an electrolyte solution of 0.1 M PBS and 5 mM K$_4$[Fe(CN)]$_6$ by EIS. The Nyquist plot typically consists of a high frequency region indicated by a semicircle, followed by a straight line at low frequency region. The diameter of the semicircle gives the R$_{ct}$. The low value of R$_{ct}$ signifies high conductivity of the electrode. Figure 3.5 depicts the Nyquist plot of bare GCE and FeTiO$_3$/GCE at their OCV. The equivalent circuit was shown in the inset of Figure 3.5.

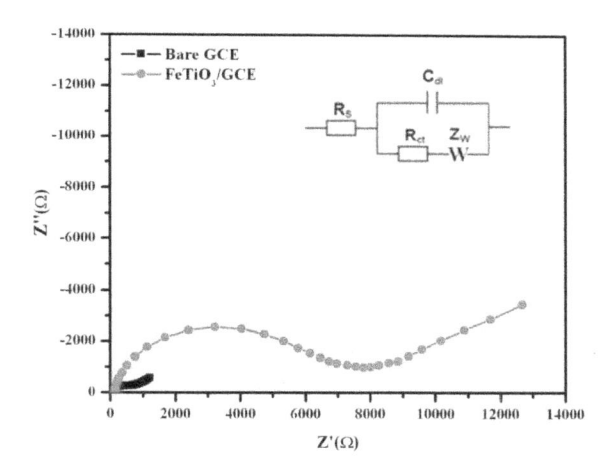

Figure 3.5. Nyquist Plot for Bare GCE and FeTiO$_3$/GCE Recorded from a Solution of 0.1 M PBS and 5 mM K$_4$[Fe(CN)$_6$] in the Frequency Range of 10^6 Hz to 0.01 Hz

The R$_{ct}$ for bare GCE was found to be 1171.00 Ω and that of FeTiO$_3$/GCE is 6949.00 Ω. In addition, the impedance spectrum was also used to calculate the degree of surface coverage of FeTiO$_3$ on GCE (Gao *et al.* 2013) using the following equation

$$\theta = 1 - \frac{R_{ct}^{bare}}{R_{ct}^{FeTiO_3}} \tag{3.1}$$

where R_{ct}^{bare} and R_{ct}^{FeTiO3} are charge transfer resistance (Ω) of bare GCE and FeTiO₃/GCE, respectively. Substituting the R_ct values in the equation, θ was calculated to be 83.15 %, which clearly confirms large surface coverage of FeTiO₃ on GCE.

3.3.2 Electro-oxidation of DA on FeTiO₃/GCE

Figure 3.6 depicts the schematic representation for electrooxidation of DA, wherein initially the adsorption of DA on FeTiO₃ takes place due to the electrostatic force of attraction. This is followed by the oxidation process with respect to the applied potential.

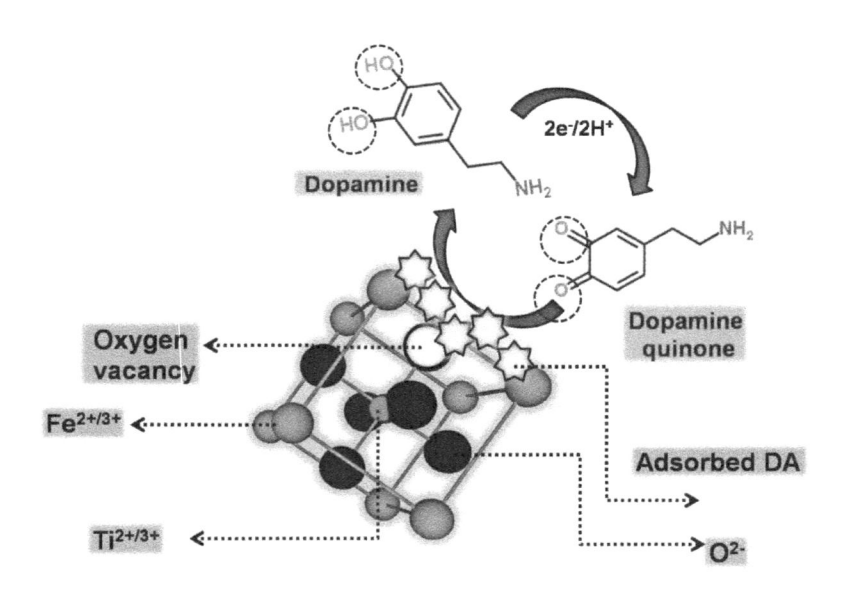

Figure 3.6. Electrooxidation of DA on FeTiO₃

The oxidation of DA is a two proton coupled two electron transfer process. To illustrate the electro-catalytic activity of the FeTiO₃/GCE, CV studies were performed in an electrolyte solution of 0.1 M PBS and 0.1 mM DA at a scan rate of 100 mV s^{-1}. Figure 3.7 shows the CV response on FeTiO$_3$/GCE in presence and absence of DA recorded in the potential region of 0 V to 0.8 V and the inset shows the CV response for DA on bare GCE. In the absence of DA, the CV curves showed the redox features of FeTiO$_3$ at around 0.6 V which also indicates its pseudocapacitive behaviour. With the addition of DA, a pair of well defined redox peak was observed on FeTiO$_3$/GCE. The forward peak corresponds to the oxidation of DA to DQ and the reverse peak corresponds to the reduction. It is seen that the oxidation current on FeTiO$_3$/GCE is higher compared to bare GCE which signifies a fast electron transfer reaction. Despite having high R$_{ct}$ compared to bare GCE, the FeTiO$_3$/GCE showed significant catalytic activity, which is attributed to the large surface area of the nanostructure, availability of oxygen deficient sites and the presence of multiple redox states of Fe and Ti. Such kind of enhanced catalytic activity was also reported for LaFeO$_3$ modified electrode (Vijayaraghavan *et al*. 2017).

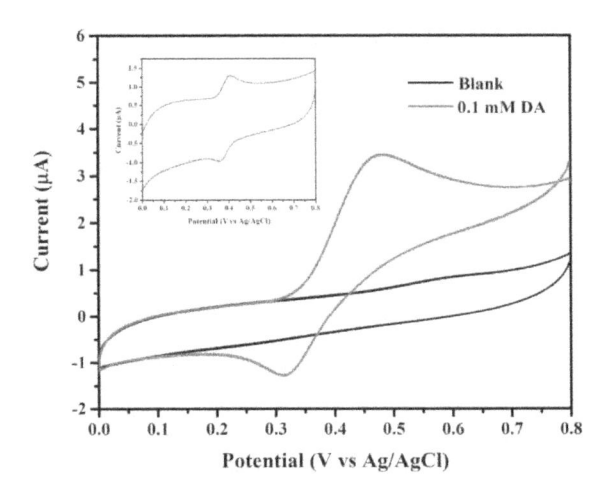

Figure 3.7. Cyclic Voltammogramm Depicting the Response of DA on FeTiO$_3$/GCE from a Solution of 0.1 M PBS and 0.1 mM of DA at a Scan Rate of 100 mV s^{-1}. The Inset Depicts the Response of bare GCE under Identical Condition

In order to comprehend the electrode kinetics, the CV curves were recorded at different scan rate. Figure 3.8a shows the CV response for 0.1 mM DA on FeTiO$_3$/GCE at different scan rate from 100 mV s^{-1} to 1000 mV s^{-1}. With increasing scan rate, the anodic and cathodic peak current values increased linearly, which indicates that, oxidation of dopamine is an adsorption controlled process. The corresponding calibration plot is shown in Figure 3.8 b.

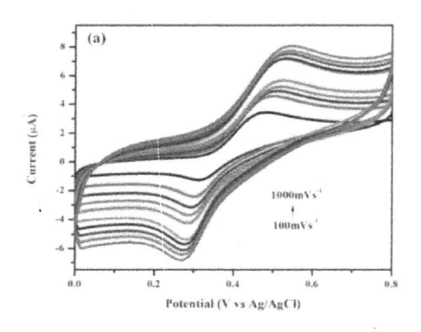

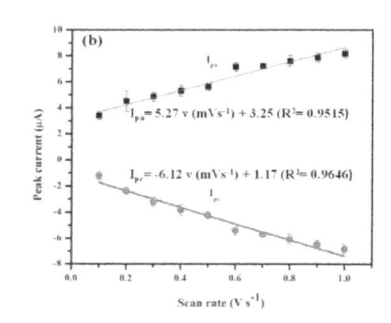

Figure 3.8. (a) CV Response of FeTiO$_3$/GCE for 0.1 mM DA at Different Scan Rates and (b) the Corresponding Calibration Plot

3.3.3 Calculation of Number of Electrons Transferred (n) and Catalytic Rate Constant (k$_{cat}$)

The n value was calculated using Laviron's equation given as follows (Laviron *et al.* 1974 and 1979).

$$I_p = nFQ\upsilon/4RT \tag{3.2}$$

where I$_p$ is the anodic peak current (A), Q is the charge corresponding to the oxidation (C), υ is the scan rate (V s^{-1}), R is the gas constant (8.314 J K^{-1} mol^{-1}) and T the temperature respectively (K). From eq (1) the value of n was deduced as 1.91 which is ~2 indicating that the oxidation of dopamine is two electron transfer process. Further, the catalytic rate constant for the oxidation of DA on

FeTiO₃/GCE was studied using CA. The CA response curves were recorded in the absence and presence of 0.15 mM DA at an applied potential of 0.15 V in 0.1 M PBS as shown in Figure 3.9 a. The catalytic rate constant (k_cat) was calculated using the equation given below (Gao *et al.* 2013)

$$\frac{I_{cat}}{I_L} = (\pi k_{cat} C_0 t)^{1/2} \qquad (3.3)$$

where I_{cat} is the catalytic current (A) of the FeTiO₃/GCE in the presence of DA, I_L is the limiting current (A) in the absence of DA, and C₀ and t are the substrate concentration (mol L⁻¹) and time (s) of analysis, respectively. Figure 3.9 b shows the linear relationship in a plot of I_cat/I_L versus t^(1/2) in the time range of 3.5 s to 3.9 s. The k_cat estimated from the slope was found to be 2.946 × 10³ M⁻¹ s⁻¹, which indicates the significant catalytic reaction of FeTiO₃/GCE compared to bare GCE.

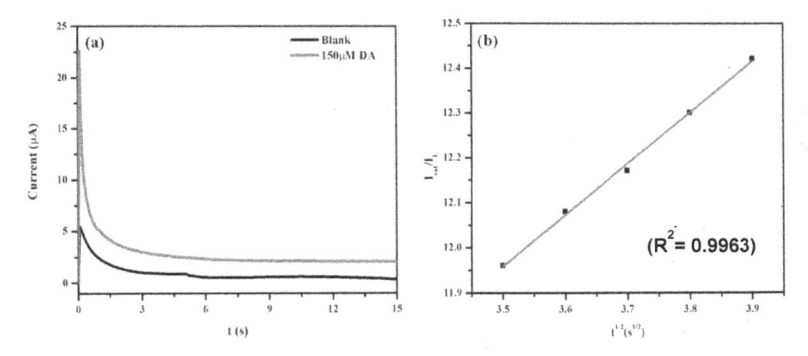

Figure 3.9. (a) CA Response of FeTiO₃/GCE in the Presence and Absence of DA at an Applied Potential of 0.15 V and (b) Depicts the Plot between t^(1/2) vs I_cat/I_L

3.3.4 pH Dependent Sensing of DA on FeTiO₃/GCE

The electrooxidation of DA is a pH sensitive reaction. In order to study the effect of pH on FeTiO₃/GCE, the DPV analysis was performed for DA at different pH in 0.1 M PBS solution. Figure 3.10 a shows the DPV response for DA at a pH range of 4 to 9 and the corresponding plot of pH vs I_{pa} and pH vs E_{pa} was depicted in Figure 3.10 b. It is seen that the peak potential decreased with increasing pH with a slope of 79 mV. Also a high peak current was obtained at pH 7.2 which is close to physiological pH of human body. Hence all the experiments were carried out at the similar pH.

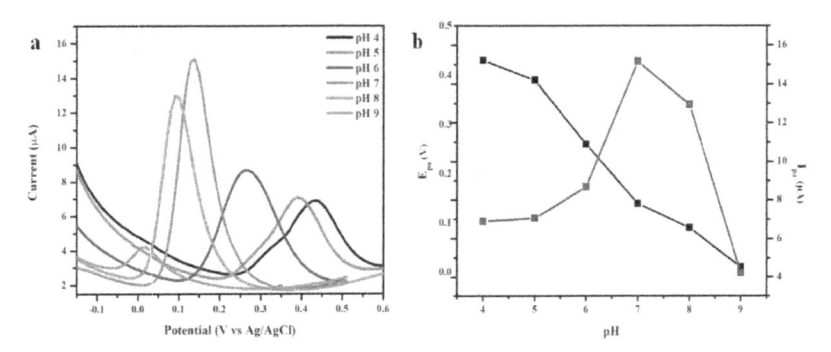

Figure 3.10. (a) DPV Response for DA on FeTiO$_3$/GCE at a pH Range of 4 to 9 from a 0.1 M PBS Solution and (b) the Variation of E_{pa} and I_{pa} with Respect to pH

3.3.5   DPV Analysis

The electrochemical detection of DA was carried out using DPV on FeTiO$_3$/GCE from a solution of 0.1 M PBS in the potential region between -0.2 V to 0.5 V. Figure 3.11a shows the DPV curves recorded for various concentration of DA and Figure 3.11b shows the corresponding calibration plot obtained by plotting concentration vs peak current. The peak current steadily increased with incremental DA levels in the electrolyte. The concentration was varied from 1 μM to 350 μM. The detection limit was estimated to be 1.3 nM and linear range was observed from 1 μM to 90 μM and 110 μM to 350 μM. The sensitivity was calculated from the slope of the calibration plot which is found to be 1.56 μA μM^{-1} cm^{-2}. Two different linear ranges were obtained with increase in DA concentration which is due to the concentration polarization effects. Similarly, the response of the FeTiO$_3$/GCE towards UA oxidation was also demonstrated as shown in Figure 3.11c. The LOD was calculated using the formula LOD=3s/m where s is the standard deviation of blank and m is the slope of the calibration curve. The detection limit was estimated to be 30 nM with linearity in the range of 1 µM to 150 µM and 200 µM to 500 µM from the calibration curve (Figure 3.11d) and a sensitivity of 0.067 µA µM^{-1} cm^{-2}.

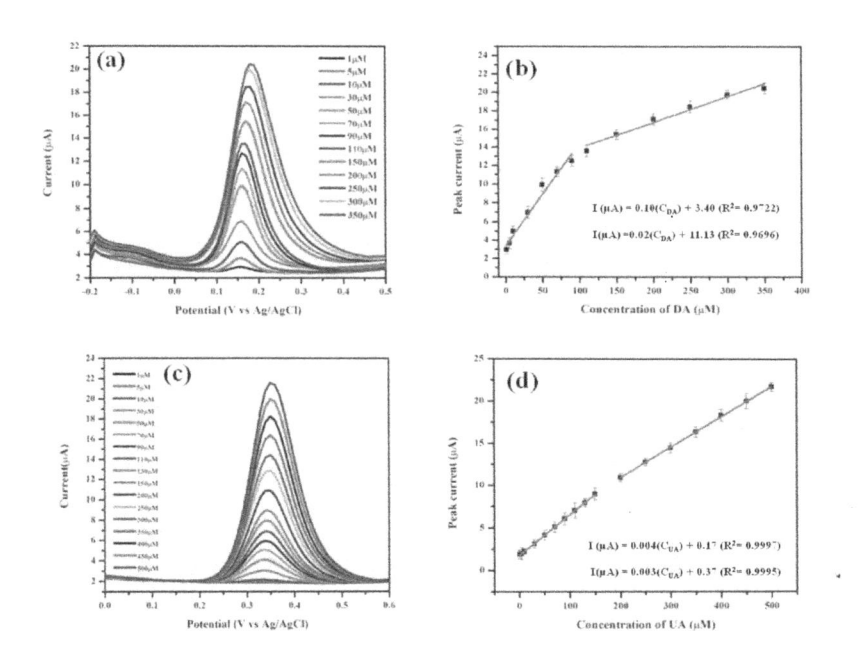

Figure 3.11. DPV Curves for (a) DA (1 µM to 350 µM) and (c) UA (1 µM to 500 µM) on FeTiO$_3$/GCE from a Solution of 0.1 M PBS, (b)&(d) shows the Corresponding Calibration Plot

The performance of the FeTiO$_3$/GCE in the electrochemical detection of DA and UA is compared with other perovskites modified electrode as shown in Table 3.1. It is seen that, the present sensor showed low detection limit among other perovskite based electrodes reported so far. For example, the detection limit obtained in this work is very low compared to LaFeO$_3$/GCE

(Thirumalairajan *et al.* 2014) and LaCoO₃/GCE (Priyatharshni *et al.* 2017). However the linear range is too short compared to other modified electrodes (Wang *et al.* 2009) which requires further improvement.

Table 3.1. A Comparative Performance of Various Perovskite Modified Electrode for DA Sensing

S. No	Electrode	Linear Range (µM)	Limit of Detection (µM)	Peak Separation (mV) (DA-UA)	Ref
1	LaFeO₃/GCE	0.15-800	0.03	130	(Wang *et al.* 2009)
2	CPE/SrPdO₃	7-70, 90-160	0.0093, 0.025	144	(Atta *et al.* 2014)
3	LaFeO₃/GCE	0.02-1.6	0.059	95	(Thirumalairajan *et al.* 2014)
4	LaFeO₃/GCE	10-100, 120-180	0.01	130	(Vijayaraghavan *et al.* 2017)
5	LaCoO₃/GCE	-	3.53	173	(Priyatharshni *et al.* 2017)
6	FeTiO₃/GCE	1-90, 110-350	0.0013	212	Present work

3.3.6 Selective and Simultaneous Detection of DA and UA

It is well known that UA interferes in the detection of DA as they oxidize at the same potential similar to DA. DPV was carried out in order to demonstrate the selective determination of DA in presence of UA. Figure 3.12a shows the DPV curves for 50 µM DA and varying concentration of UA from 50 µM to 250 µM on FeTiO₃/GCE. It is seen that the oxidation of UA occurred at ~0.35 V which is clearly distinct from that of DA. Hence, DA can be selectively determined in the presence of UA. The corresponding calibration plot was shown in Figure 3.12b.

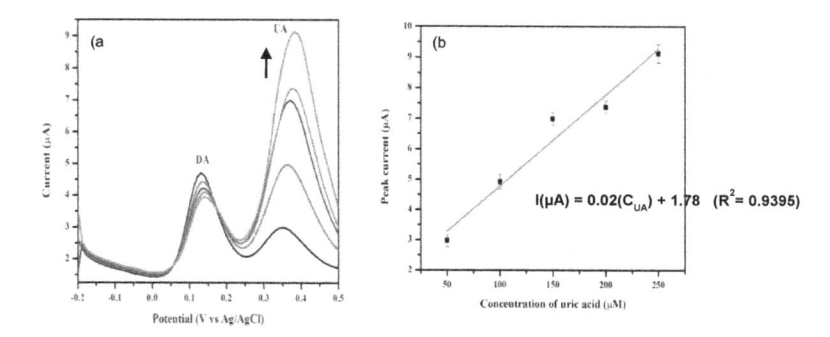

Figure 3.12.(a) DPV Response of DA in Presence of Various Concentration of UA (50 μM to 250 μM) and (b) their Corresponding Calibration Curve

In order to prove the simultaneous detection capability of the FeTiO$_3$/GCE, the DPV studies were carried out by adding equvimolar concentration of DA and UA. Figure 3.13a shows the DPV response for varying concentration of DA and UA ranging from 10 μM to 500 μM on FeTiO$_3$/GCE in 0.1 M PBS. Two distinct peaks corresponding to DA and UA were noticed with a peak to peak separation of 212 mV. This clearly enunciates the possibility of detecting DA and UA simultaneously. Figure 3.13 (b and c) shows the corresponding calibration plot for DA and UA respectively. In addition, the DPV response for DA in presence of interfering agents was analyzed. It is seen that, no significant changes were observed even with the presence of two-fold excess concentration of glucose, KCl, KNO$_3$, urea, (NH$_4$)$_2$SO$_4$, hydroxylamine, FeSO$_4$ and CuCl$_2$ solution (Figure 3.14a).

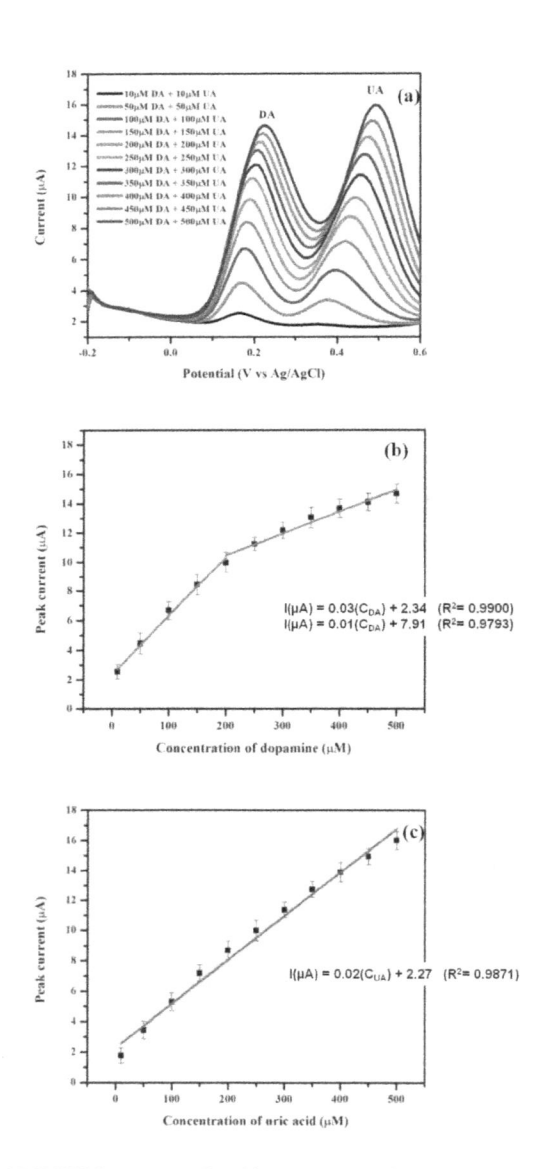

Figure 3.13.(a) DPV Response for Simultaneous Detection of DA and UA for Various Concentrations on FeTiO$_3$/GCE in 0.1 M PBS and (b) & (c) their Corresponding Calibration Plots

3.3.7 Stability and Reproducibility Studies

The repeatability of the FeTiO$_3$/GCE was evaluated from the CV studies by observing the change in peak current for DA oxidation recorded from a solution of 0.1 mM DA and 0.1 M PBS for 75 successive cycles at a scan rate of 100 mV s^{-1}. Figure 3.14b shows the CV curves recorded for the first and last cycle respectively. 11.5% decrease in peak current was noticed at the end of 75th cycle.

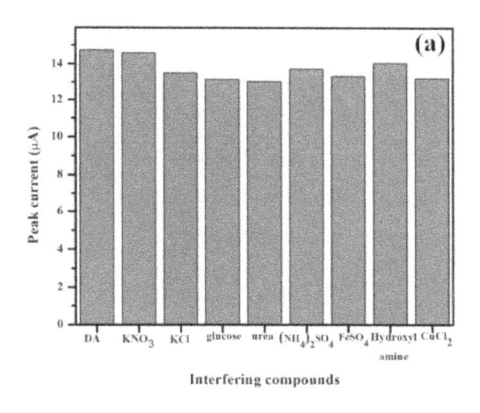

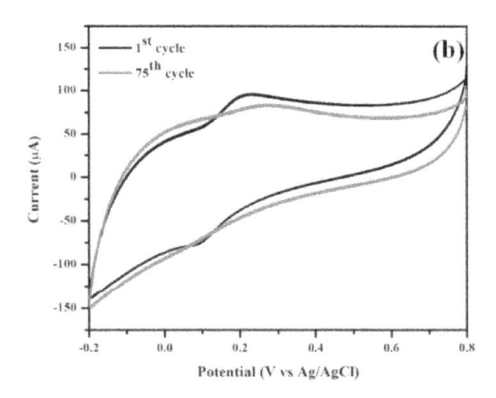

Figure 3.14. (a) Bar Plot Depicting the Variation of Peak Current for DA Detection in Presence of Various Interfering Agents and (b) the CV Response of 0.1 mM DA for the 1st and 75th Cycle

The stability of FeTiO$_3$/GCE was studied by monitoring the DPV peak current recorded for 0.1 mM DA at an interval of 2 days. The FeTiO$_3$/GCE was stored in PBS buffer after each measurement. The electrode was able to retain 80% of the initial current at the end of a week. These studies indicate the excellent stability and reproducibility of the proposed sensor.

3.3.8 Estimation of DA and UA in Human Biological Samples

The validity of the FeTiO$_3$/GCE in real samples such as serum and urine was analysed by adding a known amount of DA and UA to the solution. The accuracy and precision of the proposed method was demonstrated using three different concentrations. The obtained peak current values were compared with the calibration curve obtained in Figure 3.11b. A satisfactory percentage of recovery ranging from 80% to 110% was observed with negligible standard deviation as shown in Table 3.2.

Table 3.2. DA and UA Estimation in Human Biological Samples using FeTiO$_3$/GCE

	Amount of DA added (μM)	Amount of DA predicted (μM)	% of recovery	Amount of UA added (μM)	Amount of UA predicted (μM)	% of recovery
Serum	50	55.2	110.4±1	50	46.75	93.5
	100	82.2	82.2±3	100	85.93	85.93
	150	106	70.6±1	150	145.37	96.91
Urine	10	8.90	89±2	50	47.3	94.6
	30	27.83	92.76±1	100	104.86	104.86
	50	45.42	90.84±1	150	168.03	112.02

3.4 SUMMARY

To summarise, FeTiO$_3$ perovskite nanostructure was proposed for the electrochemical detection of DA. The nanostructure was prepared by hydrothermal method, without employing any structure directing agent. The TEM analysis indicates the presence of nanohexagons and the ilmenite structure was confirmed through XRD. XPS confirms the formation of the constituent elements and the chemical nature was analysed using FTIR spectroscopy. The modified electrode showed good catalytic activity towards DA. The detection was carried out using DPV which showed a detection limit of 1.3 nM and linear range of 1 µM to 90 µM and 110 µM to 350 µM respectively. In addition, the detection limit of UA was found to be 30 nM. The sensor showed excellent stability and reproducibility. The validity of the proposed sensor was examined in human biological samples. The low detection limit, high selectivity in presence of interfering agents, good stability and reproducibility are the advantages of the present sensor.

CHAPTER 4

STUDIES ON THE ELECTROCHEMISTRY OF DOPAMINE ON FeTiO$_3$ MODIFIED GLASSY CARBON ELECTRODE

4.1 INTRODUCTION

In the previous chapter, FeTiO$_3$ nanohexagons were tested for their efficacy in the detection of DA (Aparna *et al.* 2019). The sensor exhibited good performance in terms of sensitivity and selectivity. To study the electrochemistry of DA at FeTiO$_3$/GCE, the redox reaction of DA at FeTiO$_3$/GCE was investigated in this chapter using several electrochemical techniques such as CV, hydrodynamic voltammetry and impedance spectroscopy. The electron transfer kinetics of FeTiO$_3$/GCE was compared with bare GCE.

During the past few decades, CME using nanomaterials were reported to improve the sensor performance (Immanuel *et al.* 2018). Several metals (Pinho *et al.* 2012), metal oxides (Aparna *et al.* 2018), graphene based composites (Sivasubramanian *et al.* 2016), spinels (Aparna *et al.* 2018) and perovskites based nanostructures (Durai *et al.* 2019 and Thirumalairajan *et al.* 2012) were studied in this context. However, not much attention has been paid to analyse the electrochemistry of DA on CME including their oxidation pathways. The oxidation of DA undergoes several pathways/mechanism and the ambiguity on the exact mechanism is still under debate. It is of interest to study the redox reaction of DA on perovskite modified electrodes.

4.2 MATERIALS AND METHODS

4.2.1 Synthesis of FeTiO$_3$ Nanohexagons

The detailed synthesis and characterization of FeTiO$_3$ nanohexagons is provided in the Section 3.2.2 and Section 3.2.3 respectively in Chapter 3.

4.2.2 Electrochemical Measurements

The pre-treatment and electrode modification was carried out as per the procedure indicated in Section 3.2.4 in Chapter 3. All the electrochemical experiments were carried out from a solution of 0.5 mM DA and 0.1 M PBS solutions.

4.3 RESULTS AND DISCUSSION

4.3.1 Electrochemical behaviour of DA on FeTiO$_3$/GCE

Figure 4.1 shows the CV curves pertaining to the redox reaction of DA on FeTiO$_3$/GCE from a solution of 0.5 mM DA and 0.1 M PBS at a scan rate of 50 mV s^{-1}. The potential was scanned in the range of -1.0 V to +1.0 V vs. Ag/AgCl (3M KCl) at a pH of 7.2. Two successive voltammograms were depicted in Figure 4.1. The first cycle showed an oxidation peak (a) at 0.35 V which corresponds to the oxidation of DA to DQH. During the reverse scanning, the corresponding reduction peak appears at a' due to the reduction of DQH. Interestingly, as the potential is scanned further, redox peaks appear at b (-0.11 V) and b" (-0.38 V) respectively.

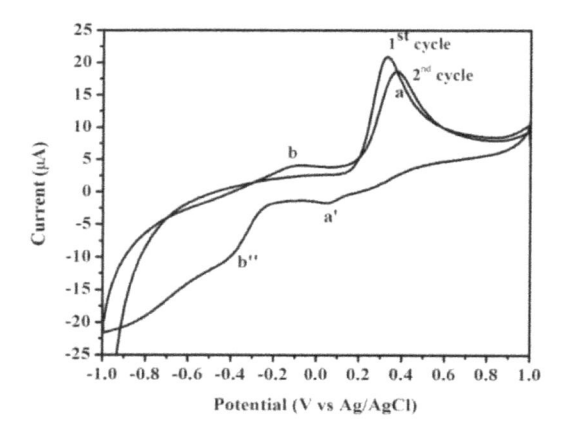

Figure 4.1. Cyclic Voltammogram Depicting the First and Second Cycle Obtained for the Redox Reaction of 0.5 mM DA in 0.1 M PBS at a Scan Rate of 50 mV s^{-1}

It is well known that, the oxidation of DA is a two electron/proton transfer process to DQH. The amine group in DQH loses a proton and forms a cyclized product LDC via 1,4-Michael addition. LDC further undergoes oxidation via two electron/proton transfer to form DC. Thus the peaks a and a' are assigned to oxidation of DA to DQH and b and b" are assigned to oxidation of LDC to DC as shown in Figure 4.1. It is to be noted that the peak b is absent during the first cycle, implying the absence of LDC at the beginning of the analysis. Also, the cathodic peak current (a') is smaller than the anodic peak current (a) indicating that, only a part of DQ gets reduced and the rest is used for the parallel reactions (steps 2,3 and 5 in Figure 1.4). These findings indicate that, the oxidation of DA on FeTiO$_3$ follows an ECE pathway. The peak separation between a and a' / b and b" are 324 mV and 259 mV respectively. This concludes the quasi-reversible nature of DA oxidation consistent with earlier studies (Vatrál *et al.* 2015). Also, it can be inferred that, the peak separation of b/b' is less than a/a', which indicates the oxidation kinetics of LDC is more easily carried out compared to the oxidation of DA. As mentioned earlier, the ambiguity over the oxidation of DA is still not clear as they proceed either via ECC or ECE pathway. Several reports are available in literature in this context (Zhang *et al.* 1993 and Palomäki *et al.* 2015). In the present case, the results from CV studies show that oxidation should proceed through an electrochemical coupled chemical pathway. Figure 4.2 depicts the effect of scan rate on the oxidation of DA at pH 7.2.

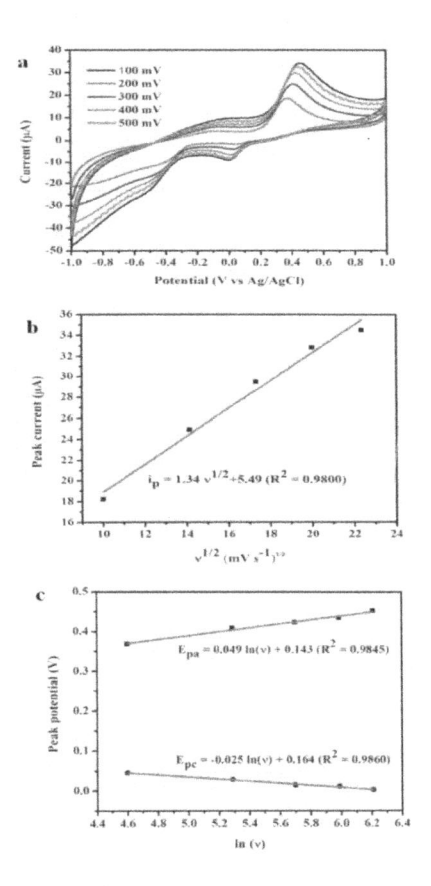

Figure 4.2. (a) Cyclic Voltmmograms Obtained for the Redox Reaction of 0.5 mM DA in 0.1 M PBS at Different Scan Rate from 100 mV s^{-1} to 500 mV s^{-1}; (b) the Corresponding Plot between Peak Current *vs* v^{½} and (c) Plot between ln (v) *vs* Peak Potential

Figure 4.2a shows the CV curves obtained for the redox reaction of DA at various scan rates ranging from 100 mV s^{-1} to 500 mV s^{-1} and Figure 4.2b showed the plot of DA oxidation peak current with respect to v$^{1/2}$. The plot showed a linear relationship indicating that the oxidation of DA is a diffusion controlled process. i.e. the diffusion of DA is the rate limiting step. At lower scan rates 10 and 50 mV s^{-1} shown in the Figure 4.3, the reduction peak of DQH is not clearly visible, indicating the rate of intramolecular cyclization is faster leading to passivation. However, on moving to higher scan rates, the reduction peak becomes clearly visible, which means the cyclization reaction does not have enough time to occur. This can be further confirmed from the increasing I_{pc}/I_{pa} ratio with scan rate as shown in Table 4.1. Also, a significant increase in ΔE_p was observed with increase in scan rate.

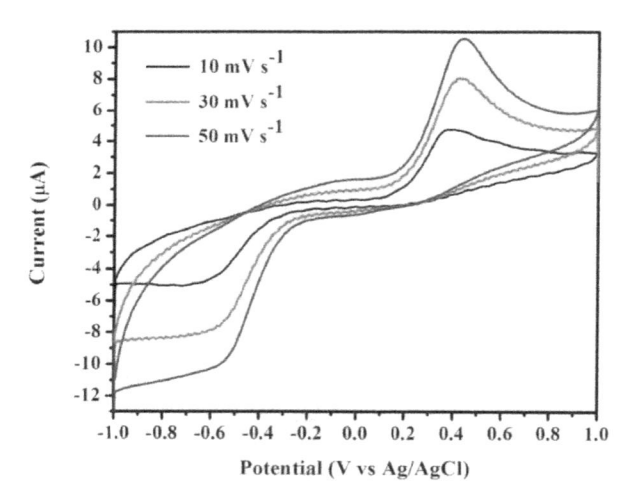

Figure 4.3. CV Corresponding to the Redox Reaction of DA on FeTiO$_3$/GCE at Scan Rate Ranging from 10 mV s^{-1} to 50 mV s^{-1}

Table 4.1. Peak Potential Separation and Peak Current Ratio for 0.5 mM DA at pH 7 at Different Scan Rate

Scan Rate (mV/s)	$I_{a'}$ (µA)	I_a (µA)	$I_b/I_{b''}$	ΔE_p (mV)
100	-1.67	18.84	0.08	326
200	-3.92	24.72	0.15	387
300	-6.28	29.94	0.20	420
400	-7.79	32.88	0.23	446
500	-8.75	34.66	0.25	452

In order to determine the kinetic parameters such as number of electron transferred, transfer coefficient and heterogeneous rate constant, Lavirons's equation (Laviron *et al.* 1974 and 1979) was employed as given below.

$$E_{pa} = E^{o'} + \frac{RT}{(1-\alpha)nF} \ln \frac{(1-\alpha)nF}{RTk_s} + \frac{RT}{(1-\alpha)nF} \ln v \quad (4.1)$$

$$E_{pc} = E^{o'} - \frac{RT}{\alpha nF} \ln \frac{\alpha nF}{RTk_s} - \frac{RT}{\alpha nF} \ln v \quad (4.2)$$

$$\Delta E_p = \frac{RT}{(1-\alpha)\alpha nF} [\alpha \ln(1-\alpha) + (1-\alpha)\ln\alpha - \frac{RT}{nF} - \ln k_s] + \frac{RT}{(1-\alpha)\alpha nF} \ln v \quad (4.3)$$

where ΔE_p is the peak potential separation (V), n is the number of electrons transferred, α is the transfer coefficient, F is Faraday constant (96485 C/mol), k_s is the heterogeneous rate constant (cm s^{-1}), v is the scan rate (V s^{-1}), R is the gas constant (8.314 J K^{-1} mol^{-1}) and T is the temperature (K). From the slope and intercept of the plot E vs. ln (v) (Figure 4.2c), the number of electrons transferred was found to be 1.89 and the electron transfer rate constant was estimated to be 0.0030 cm s^{-1}. Similar rate constant was also reported earlier on carbon paste electrode (Corona-Avendaño et al. 2007). The role of SDS on the oxidation of DA was investigated and it is noted that the heterogeneous rate constant increases when the concentration of SDS is greater than the critical micelle concentration. Also, low heterogeneous rate constant was observed in the case of other perovskite based sensor reported earlier (Thirumalairajan et al. 2012 and 2014). In addition, the transfer coefficient was found to be 0.76 indicating a quasi-reversible behaviour for DA oxidation on FeTiO$_3$/GCE.

4.3.2 Effect of pH on Redox Reaction of DA

The pH dependence of the redox reaction of DA on FeTiO$_3$/GCE is shown in Figure 4.4a. The DA response for various pH ranging from 3 to 11 was recorded at a scan rate of 50 mV s^{-1}. The potential shifted towards negative with the increase in pH. Also at pH 9 and 11, the peak at ~ -0.6 V corresponding to LDC redox couple is well defined. This is because the intracyclization of DQH takes place preferably at more alkaline pH. Literature reports also indicate that self polymerization of DA occurs in alkaline solution on various substrates leading to the formation of polydopamine films (Schindler et al. 2019).

The formation of such polydopamine film leads to passivation of electrode surface. DA oxidizes to DC which isomerizes to 5,6-hydroxy indole and further oxidizes to poly(5,6-indole quinone) on a gold substrate (Li et al. 2006). However, the mechanism of polydopamine formation is still unclear. The peak potential and peak current values for the redox reaction of DA at different pH were shown in Table 4.2. The ΔE_p value was found to decrease with the change of pH from 3 to 11. Further, the plot of formal potential $E^{o'}$ vs pH was constructed (Figure 4.4b) and slope of 49 mV/pH was obtained, which again indicates that the oxidation is a two electron coupled two proton process.

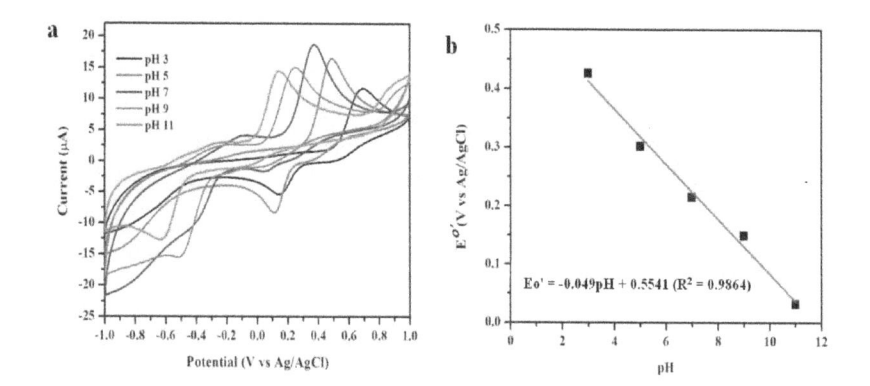

Figure 4.4. (a) CV Curves Recorded for the Redox Reaction of DA at Different pH and (b) the Plot between Formal Potential (E$^{o'}$) vs pH

Table 4.2. Redox Potentials and Peak Currents Estimated from Cyclic Voltammetry at Different pH

H	$I_p^a{}_a$ (μA)	$I_p^c{}_{a'}$ (μA)	$I_p^c{}_b$ (μA)	$I_p^a{}_{b''}$ (μA)	$\Delta E_{p\,(a/a')}$ (mV)	$\Delta E_{p\,(b/b'')}$ (mV)
3	11.62	-5.19	1.06	-7.35	547	690
5	16.55	-8.51	1.40	-10.48	371	732
7	18.55	-1.57	4.02	-10.64	315	515
9	15.09	-0.90	2.40	-15.75	217	251
11	14.26	-1.08	3.04	-12.62	101	350

Figure 4.5a depicts the CV curves recorded for the redox reaction of DA on FeTiO$_3$ for 25 continuous cycles. It can be observed that, the peak current decreases gradually from the initial 1st cycle to 25th cycle. Also, the peak separation increases and decrease in the peak current was noted with successive potential cycles. At the end of 25th cycle, the CV curve looks flat with no characteristic features. These results support the formation of melanin-like polymer (polydopamine) (Dreyer *et al.* 2013) which was further confirmed by

FTIR-ATR spectrum as shown in Figure 4.5b. Peaks at 3283 cm^{-1} and 2930 cm^{-1} can be assigned to O-H and C-H symmetric stretching vibrations respectively. The strong peak at 1538 cm^{-1} can be assigned to aromatic C=C stretching vibration. Another strong peak at 1084 cm^{-1} can be assigned to C-O group. The results were consistent with the earlier literature reports (Zangmeister *et al.* 2013).

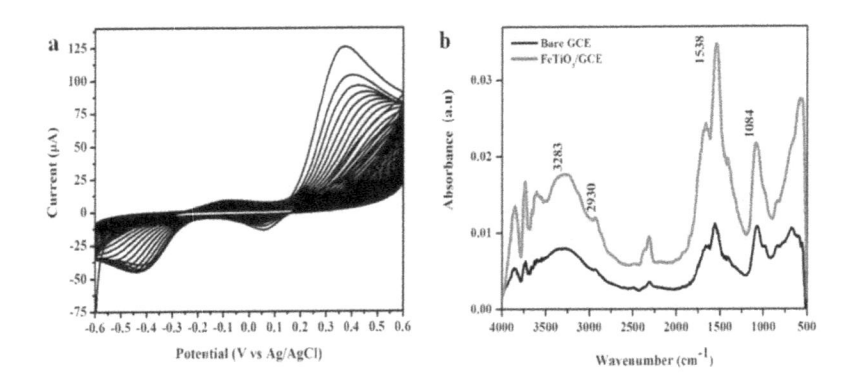

Figure 4.5. (a) CV Recorded for the Redox Reaction of DA for 25 Continuous cycles from a Solution of 0.5 mM of DA and 0.1 M PBS at a Scan Rate of 50 mV s^{-1} and (b) ATR-FTIR Studies of Polydopamine Formation on Bare GCE and FeTiO$_3$/GCE

4.3.3 Hydrodynamic Voltammetry

The kinetics of the redox reaction of DA was further probed using RDE from 0.5 mM DA and 0.1 M PBS solution. Figure 4.6a shows the RDE curves recorded at different rpm from 100 rpm to 500 rpm at a scan rate of 50 mV s^{-1}. The onset potential was observed at ~ 0.15V and the diffusion limited current increases with increasing rotation rates. In order to deduce the kinetic parameters, K-L plot was constructed based on the following equation (Bard *et al.* 2000).

$$\frac{1}{i_m} = \frac{1}{i_k} + \frac{1}{i_{MT}} = \frac{1}{nFkc} + \frac{1}{0.21\, nFD^{2/3}\, v^{-1/6}\, c\omega^{1/2}} \quad (4.4)$$

where i_m is the measured current (A), i_k is the kinetic current (A), i_{MT} is the mass transport current (A), n is the number of electrons, F is the Faraday constant (96,485 C/mol), v is the kinematic viscosity of the solution (0.01 cm^2/s), D is the diffusion coefficient, c is the bulk analyte concentration (1x 10^{-6} mol/cm^3), ω is the rotation rate of the electrode (rpm) and k is the potential dependent apparent heterogeneous electron transfer rate constant. A plot of 1/i vs 1/ω$^{1/2}$ was constructed at 0.4V as shown in Figure 4.6b and from the slope of the curve the number of electrons was calculated to be ~1.75, which is consistent with the calculation performed earlier. This further confirms that the oxidation of DA involves a two electron transfer electrochemical reaction.

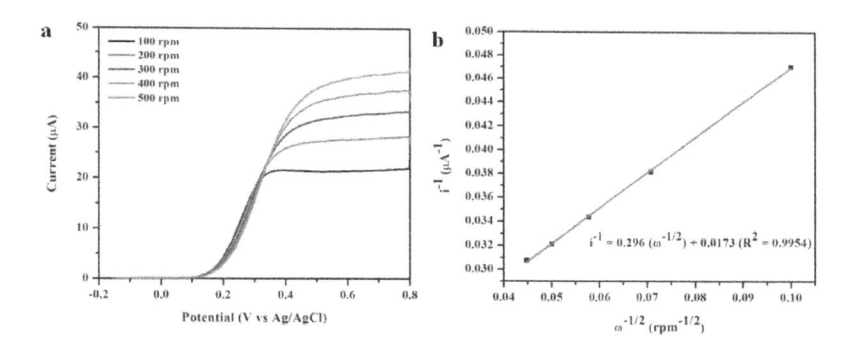

Figure 4.6. (a) RDE Curves Recorded at Different Rotation rates for the Oxidation of 0.5 mM DA in 0.1 M PBS in the Potential Range of -0.2 V to 0.8 V at a Scan of 50 mV s^{-1} and (b) their K-L Plot

4.3.4 Impedance Studies

Figure 4.7a shows the Nyquist plot recorded on FeTiO$_3$/GCE from a solution of 0.5 mM DA and 0.1 M PBS at different applied potential.

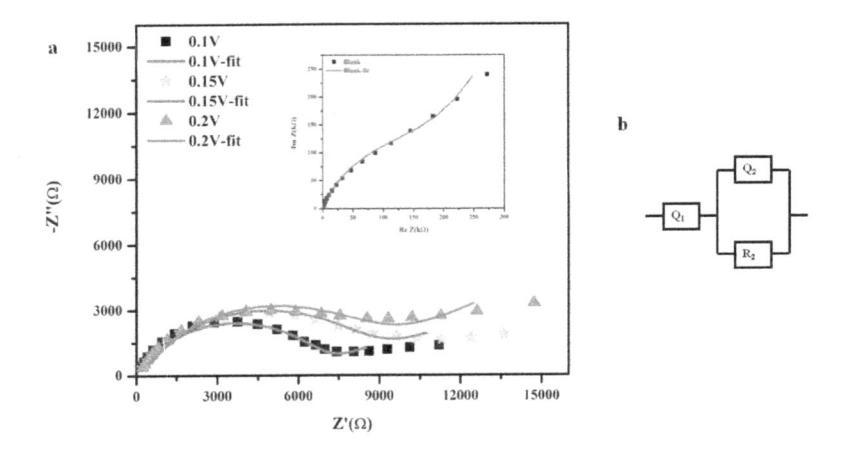

Figure 4.7. (a) Nyquist Plot Obtained for the Oxidation of DA at Different Applied Potentials; the Inset Depicts the Plot Obtained for Blank Solution (0.1 M PBS alone) at their OCP and (b) the Corresponding Electrical Equivalent Circuit

The Nyquist plot shows a semicircle at the high frequency region followed by a vertical spike at low frequency for all the potentials (Macdonald et al. 2005). The diameter of the semicircle indicates the R_{ct}. It is seen that, as the potential is increased from 0.1 V to 0.2 V, the R_{ct} increases. This increase in R_{ct} is due to the adsorption of oxidized product on the surface of the electrode which impedes further oxidation of DA with respect to applied potential. This indicates that the surface is prone to more passivation which plausibly decreases the electron transfer kinetics. However, in the absence of DA, no characteristic semicircle was obtained as shown in the inset of Figure 4.7a. The Nyquist plots were fitted with the corresponding equivalent circuit as shown in Figure 4.7b and the values are provided in Table 4.3. The fitting was performed by keeping the standard deviation (χ^2) less than 1. It model was used to fit the Nyquist plot, where Q depicts the CPE and R_2 denotes the charge transfer resistance. In Figure 4.7b, Q_1 corresponds to the inhomogenity of the electrode and Q_2 and R_2 arise due to the charge transfer across the electrode/electrolyte interface. As the potential is increased, the R_2/R_{ct} increases. The value of n typically varies from 0 to 1. From Table 4.3, it is clear that n_2 value shows a typical value near to 1, which indicates the capacitive nature of the electrode.

Table 4.3. EEC Parameters at Different Applied Potential for FeTiO$_3$/GCE

Potential (V)	R$_2$ (Ω)	Q$_1$ (μF)	Q$_2$ (μF)	n$_1$	n$_2$	C$_{dl}$ (μF)
0.1	6250	450	3.1	0.30	0.78	1.01
0.15	7250	230	2.8	0.29	0.78	0.93
0.2	7500	150	2.7	0.35	0.77	0.84

Figure 4.8 (a and b) depicts the Bode plot of log (frequency) vs. phase angle and log (frequency) vs. |z| respectively. From Figure 4.8a, it is clear that, all the applied potential showed a maximum phase angle of 65° suggesting a non-ideal capacitive behaviour, which arises mostly due to the roughness of the electrode (Chang *et al.* 2006). An angle of 45° mostly shows an ideal capacitive behaviour. Similarly, a phase angle of 75° was reported on CPE(Díaz *et al.* 2013). Figure 4.8b shows the plot of log (frequency) vs.log |z|. At high frequency region, the value seems to be almost similar. On the other hand, at low frequency, the value changes in the range of 3.6 to 4.4 for different applied potentials. The slope of the straight line was measured to be -1, indicating a capacitive behaviour of the electrode (Lojou *et al.* 2002).

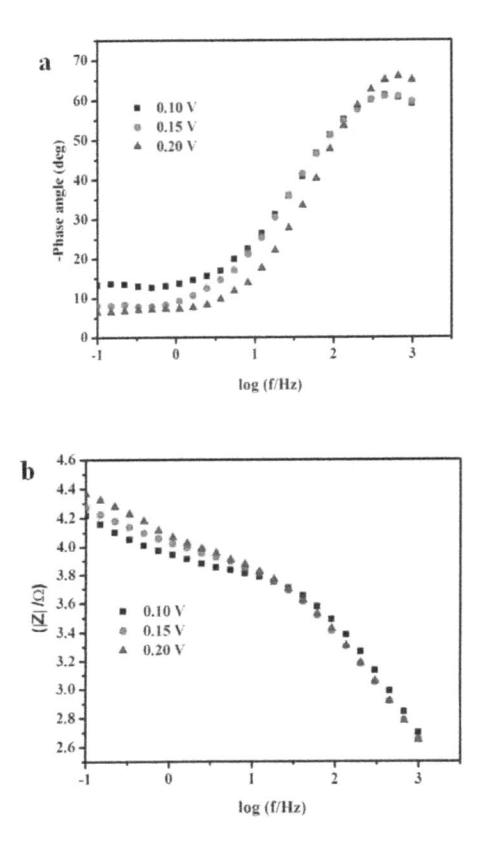

Figure 4.8. Bode Plot (a) log (f) vs Phase Angle and (b) log (f) vs |z| for the Oxidation of DA at Different Applied Potential on FeTiO₃/GCE

4.3.5 Comparison with GCE

The redox reaction of DA on FeTiO₃/GCE was studied using various electrochemical techniques and the results were compared with bare GCE. The oxidation of DA on bare GCE was recorded at pH 7.2 under the same condition. It is seen that, DA shows better response on GCE surface with well defined peaks as shown in Figure 4.9 (a and b). Moreover, the peak potential separation was less than that of FeTiO₃ indicating quasi-reversible reaction. The I_{pc}/I_{pa} ratio is less than unity, which shows an electrochemical coupled with chemical reaction pathway for the oxidation of DA. This means that, the oxidation of DA on FeTiO$_3$ follows the same path as that of bare GCE. However, the electrochemical kinetics estimated from equation (1-3) for bare GCE showed heterogeneous electron transfer rate constant to be 2.2 x 10^{-2} cm s^{-1}, with n as ~2 and transfer coefficient as 0.59. These results indicate that, despite the oxidation mechanistic pathway for FeTiO$_3$ and bare GCE are identical, bare GCE is more reversible compared to FeTiO$_3$/GCE. The results are consistent with charge transfer resistance obtained for FeTiO$_3$ and GCE on K$_4$[Fe(CN)$_6$] solution (Aparna *et al.* 2019). The high resistance of FeTiO$_3$ makes it less conducting compared to bare GCE. Despite showing an excellent performance towards the detection of DA, FeTiO$_3$ exhibit slow electron transfer kinetics compared to bare GCE.

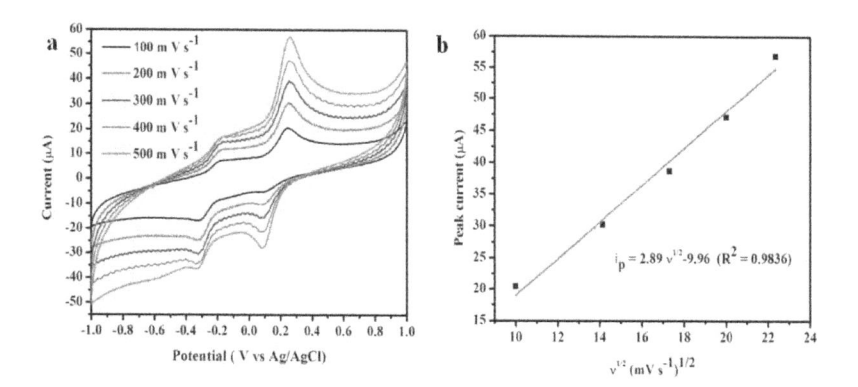

Figure 4.9. (a) CV Corresponding to the Redox Reaction of DA on Bare GCE at Scan Rate Ranging from 100 mV s^{-1} to 500 mV s^{-1} and (b) the Corresponding Plot between i$_p$ vs v^{½}

4.4 SUMMARY

The electrochemistry of DA was investigated on FeTiO$_3$/GCE using various electrochemical techniques. The CV studies revealed an electrochemical coupled chemical pathway and the oxidation apparently follows a diffusion controlled reaction. The mechanistic pathway is similar to that observed for GCE and the kinetic investigation showed sluggish electron transfer kinetics for FeTiO$_3$. The reaction is said to follow a two electron coupled two proton transfer process. The effect of pH revealed high intramolecular cyclization at alkaline pH with also a possibility of self polymerization to melanin-like compound. Further, the kinetics was also investigated using RDE. Also, it was observed that the R$_{ct}$ increases with increase in applied potential which may be due to surface passivation. Despite the excellent performance of FeTiO$_3$ in the detection of DA, it exhibits slow electron transfer kinetics compared to GCE.

CHAPTER 5

POLYDOPAMINE COATED FeTiO₃ NANOHEXAGONS FOR ELECTROCHEMICAL DETECTION OF DOPAMINE

5.1 INTRODUCTION

Considering the presence of oxygen vacancies in the crystal structure and the existence of multiple oxidation states, perovskite nanostructures are expected to be of great significance for the sensing of DA, as demonstrated in the earlier chapter. In order to improve the stability of the nanostructures a polymer coating is introduced along the FeTiO₃. For example, PNMPy hollow particles were synthesized by LbL self-assembly technique and electrochemical sensors for DA detection was prepared by coating GCE and AuNPs-GCE with PNMPy nanomembrane (Martí et al. 2010). From the results, it was observed that the sensor was able to detect DA at much lower concentrations owing to the high sensitivity of the conducting polymer PNMPy to DA. It was also found that, the sensors exhibited a fast response even at lower concentration. Polymers such as PEDOT and PDA were also used in electrochemical sensing of DA. A platinum electrode was modified with a hybrid film of PEDOT/PDA (Salgado et al. 2013). A potential step technique was used to electrpolymerize PEDOT on bare Pt electrode. PDA was then subsequently obtained on PEDOT coated electrode by means of CV. Improvement in electrochemical performance was observed after modification of materials with PDA. PDA enabled the selective detection of DA in presence of AA and UA. The sensor also showed a low LOD of 0.65 µM with a linear range from 1.5 to 50 µM.

PDA nanoparticles and films have attracted huge attention owing to their physicochemical properties. The presence of hydroxyl and amine moieties in the structure is more susceptible to oxidation and thus, at an alkaline pH, DA monomer can undergo polymerization to form a PDA polymer. PDA has an adhesive nature and it is used as a surface modification agent for various materials. PDA also exhibits zwitter ionicity and has very good ionic permeability (Gao *et al*. 2014). In this work, the $FeTiO_3$ nanohexagons were coated with PDA in a simple procedure to further improve the performance of the sensor. The study reported the electrochemical detection of DA using PDA-$FeTiO_3$/GCE. Selective and simultaneous detection of DA and UA was demonstrated and the sensor was also validated in serum and urine samples.

5.2 MATERIALS AND METHODS

5.2.1 Synthesis of $FeTiO_3$ Nanohexagons

The synthesis procedure for $FeTiO_3$ nanohexagons by hydrothermal method was described briefly in Chapter 3.

5.2.2 Synthesis of PDA Coated $FeTiO_3$ Nanocomposite

For the synthesis of PDA coated $FeTiO_3$, 200mg of $FeTiO_3$ nanohexagons synthesized earlier by hydrothermal method and 50mg of dopamine hydrochloride was added to 10 mL of 10 mM Tris buffer solution. After stirring for 2 hours at room temperature, the solution was centrifuged, washed with distilled water twice and dried at 80°C overnight (Yue *et al*. 2018).

5.2.3 Preparation of DA Stock Solutions and Real Samples

A 5 mM stock solution of DA was prepared by dissolving dopamine hydrochloride in 0.1 M PBS. From the stock, different concentrations of DA were used for the experiments. To prepare the serum and urine samples, 100 µL of the samples were diluted in 0.1 M PBS and the diluted solution was used as the electrolyte to study the detection of DA and UA.

5.2.4 Electrochemical Measurements

The GCE electrode was cleaned with alumina powder prior to material modification. FeTiO$_3$ was dropcasted on the GCE surface as per the earlier procedure (Section 3.2.4 in Chapter 3). CV experiments were carried out using PDA-FeTiO$_3$/GCE in the potential range of -0.2V to +0.8V from a solution of 0.1 mM DA and 0.1 M PBS. Similarly, the potential window for DPV was given as -0.2 V to +0.5 V. Stock solutions of DA and UA were prepared with a concentration of 5 mM. EIS was used for investigating the electrochemical kinetics of PDA-FeTiO$_3$/GCE in 5 mM K$_4$[Fe(CN)$_6$] and 0.1 M PBS at open circuit voltage (OCV) in the frequency range of 10^6 Hz to 0.01 Hz.

5.3 RESULTS AND DISCUSSION

5.3.1 Characterization of PDA-FeTiO$_3$

5.3.1.1 SEM

The surface morphologies of FeTiO$_3$ and PDA-FeTiO$_3$ were analyzed using FESEM. Figure 5.1 (a - d) shows the FESEM images of FeTiO$_3$ and PDA-FeTiO$_3$ respectively. Figure 5.1 (a and b) shows the FESEM image of FeTiO$_3$ where in hexagonal morphology is clearly visible. In the case of PDA-FeTiO$_3$, a continuous coating of PDA over FeTiO$_3$ could be seen (Figure 5.1 (c and d)). The co-ordination of catechol group of DA with Fe in FeTiO$_3$ led to increased affinity of PDA towards FeTiO$_3$.

The PDA coating was further confirmed with elemental mapping showing the presence of elements, Fe, Ti, O, C and N in the nanocomposite. Figure 5.2a shows the mapping of all elements in FeTiO$_3$ and (b, c and d) shows the presence of individual elements Fe, Ti and O respectively. Similarly, Figure 5.3a shows the mapping of all elements in PDA-FeTiO$_3$ and (b, c, d, e and f) shows the individual elements Fe, Ti, O, C and N respectively.

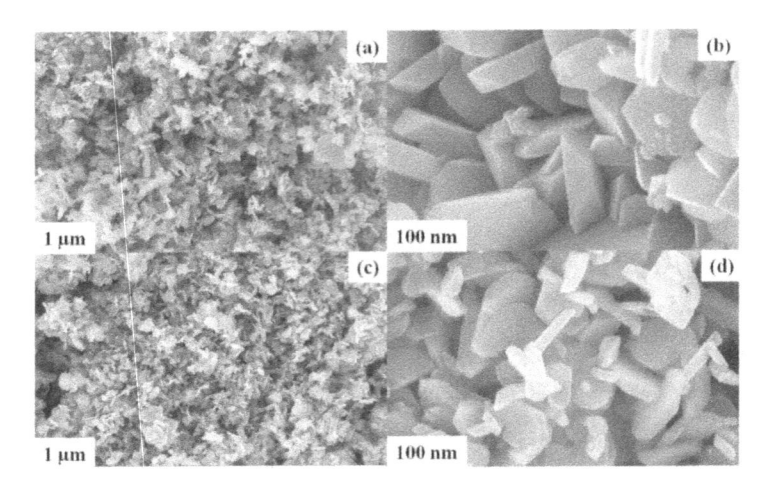

Figure 5.1. (a and b) FESEM Images of FeTiO$_3$ Recorded at Different Magnifications; (c and d) FESEM Images of PDA-FeTiO$_3$ Recorded at Different Magnifications

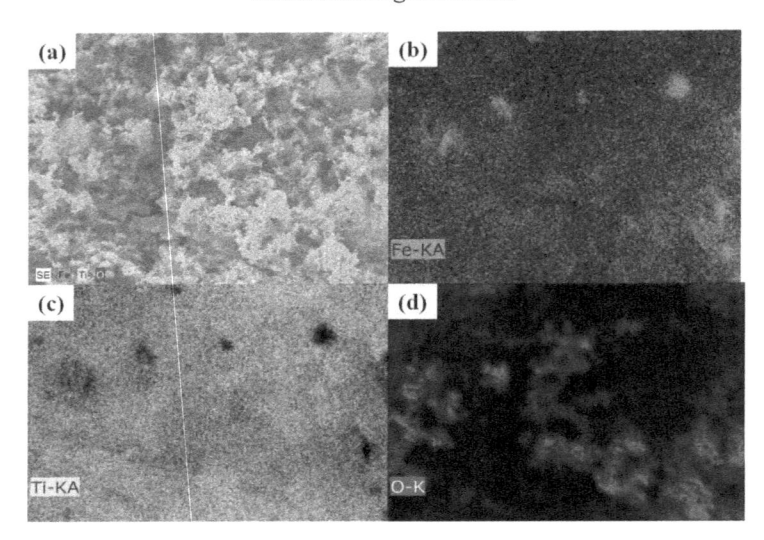

Figure 5.2. (a) Elemental Map showing the Distribution of Different Elements in FeTiO$_3$ Nanostructure; (b, c and d) Elemental Maps showing Individual Elements Fe, Ti and O Respectively

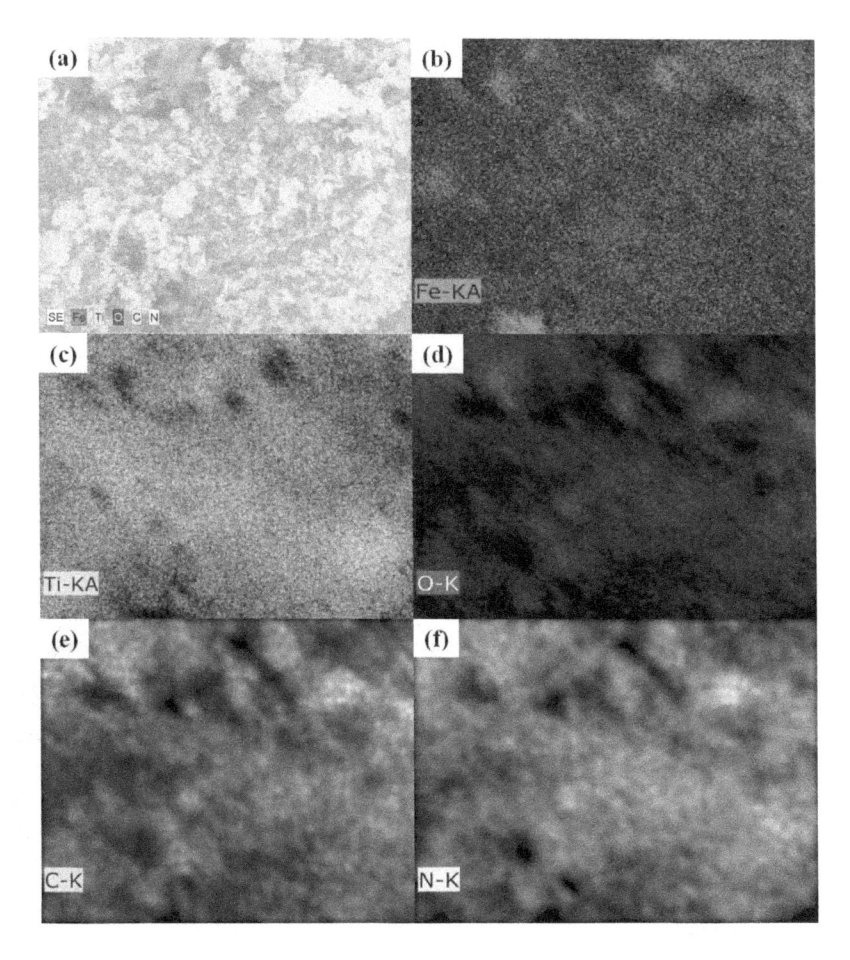

Figure 5.3. (a) Elemental Map showing the Distribution of Different Elements in PDA-FeTiO₃ Nanocomposite; (b, c and d) Elemental Maps showing Individual Elements Fe, Ti and O Respectively

5.3.1.2 TEM

TEM images of PDA-FeTiO₃ are shown in Figure 5.4. Uniform PDA polymer coating was observed around the FeTiO₃ nanohexagons. A thin coating of PDA coating around 6 nm in thickness was observed over FeTiO₃ nanohexagons.

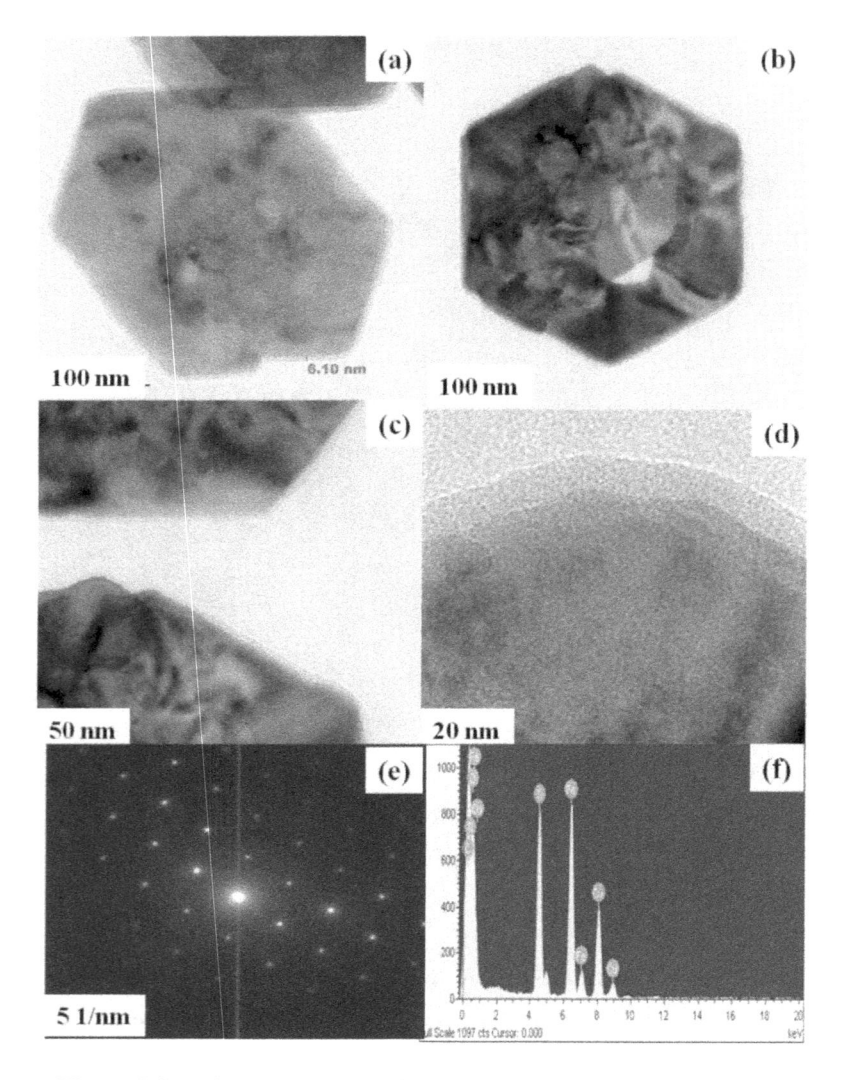

Figure 5.4. (a-d) TEM Images of PDA-FeTiO₃ Recorded at Different Magnifications; (d) the Corresponding SAED Pattern and (e) shows the EDX Image Respectively

Figure 5.4 (a and b) shows PDA-FeTiO₃ at a scale of 100 nm. Figure 5.4 (c and d) shows PDA-FeTiO₃ at a scale of 50 nm and 20 nm respectively and the electron diffraction pattern indicating the crystalline nature of FeTiO$_3$ is given in Figure 5.4e. EDX spectrum showing the presence of elements in PDA-FeTiO$_3$ is given in Figure 5.4e.

5.3.1.3 XRD

The XRD patterns of FeTiO$_3$ and PDA-FeTiO$_3$ are shown in Figure 5.5. The diffraction peaks corresponds to the ilmenite structure and is in accordance with JCPDS reference no. 29-0733 for both FeTiO$_3$ and PDA-FeTiO$_3$. The peaks at 23.8 °, 32.7 °, 35.4 °, 40.5 °, 49.1 °, 53.4 °, 62.0 ° and 63.9 ° are well indexed to (012), (104), (110), (113), (024), (116), (214) and (300) planes respectively. The PDA-FeTiO$_3$ showed an additional broad peak around 15.0 ° corresponding to the amorphous polymer PDA layer. The amorphous nature of PDA was also observed in other works reported in the literature.

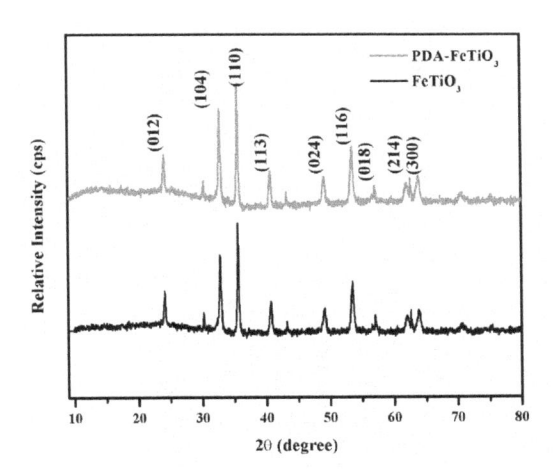

Figure 5.5. XRD Pattern of FeTiO$_3$ and PDA-FeTiO$_3$ Nanocomposite

5.3.1.4 FTIR

The FTIR spectrum for FeTiO$_3$ and PDA-FeTiO$_3$ is shown in Figure 5.6. In the case of FeTiO$_3$, two peaks at 3362 cm^{-1} and 2899 cm^{-1} corresponds to stretching vibrations of -OH and C-H groups respectively. Other peaks at 1542 cm^{-1} and 1357 cm^{-1} were observed for asymmetrical and symmetrical stretching vibrations of O-C=O respectively. At 554 cm^{-1}, the peak was attributed to Fe-O stretching vibration. The FTIR spectrum of PDA-FeTiO$_3$ shows similar peaks at 3331 cm^{-1} and 2869 cm^{-1} which corresponds to stretching vibrations of -OH and C-H respectively. However, the -OH peak is broad, which might be linked to the stretching vibration of -NH groups from PDA layer. The C-H peak was also well defined with higher intensity compared to that of FeTiO$_3$. These results confirm the PDA coating on FeTiO$_3$ nanostructure.

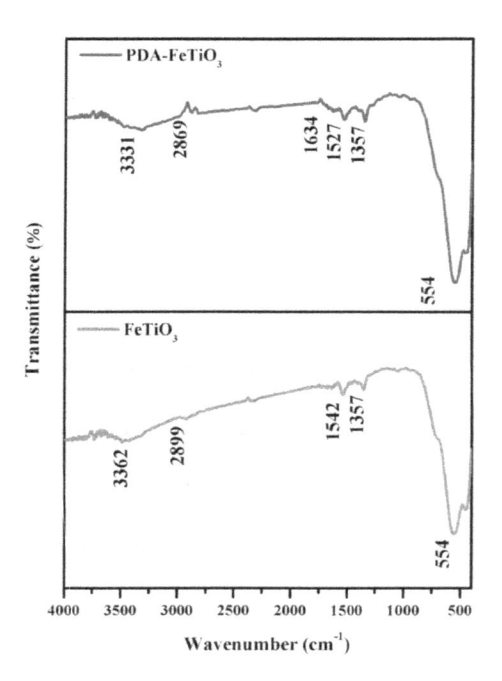

Figure 5.6. FTIR Spectrum of FeTiO$_3$ and PDA-FeTiO$_3$ Nanocomposite

5.3.1.5 XPS

Further, Figure 5.7 shows the XPS spectrum of PDA-FeTiO$_3$ nanocomposite.

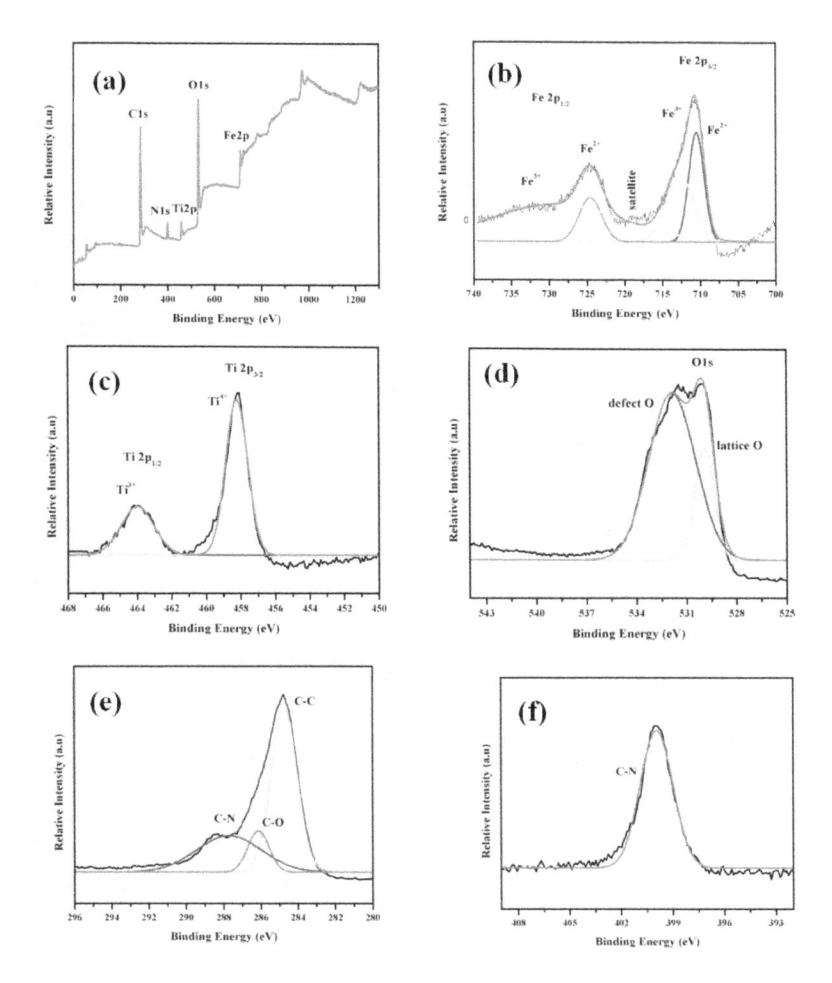

Figure 5.7. XPS Spectrum of PDA-FeTiO$_3$ (a) Survey Spectrum, (b) Fe 2p, (c) O 1s, (d) Ti 2p, (e) C 1s and (f) N 1s Respectively

Figure 5.7a shows the survey spectrum wherein the presence of all elements such as Fe 2p, Ti 2p, O 1s, C 1s and N 1s were inferred. Figure 5.7b shows the high intensity peak of Fe^{2+}. Two major peaks were noticed at 724.54 eV and 710.57 eV which corresponds to Fe $2p_{1/2}$ and Fe $2p_{3/2}$ states respectively. In addition, a small hump at 712.81 eV showed the presence of Fe^{3+}. In the case of Ti, two peaks at 463.99 eV and 458.21 eV belongs to Ti $2p_{3/2}$ and Ti $2p_{1/2}$ respectively (Figure 5.7c). Here too, the presence of Ti^{3+} and Ti^{4+} was inferred.

The deconvoluted O 1s spectrum was shown in Figure 5.7d. Two peaks at 529.91 eV and 531.79 eV corresponds to M-O and C-O bonds respectively. Also in the case of C 1s, peaks at 284.76 eV (C=C) and 286.12 eV (C=O) were revealed (Figure 5.7e). The presence of N 1s was confirmed from the peak obtained at 399.94 eV (Figure 5.7f). The above results indicate the formation of PDA-$FeTiO_3$ nanocomposite and are consistent with earlier literature reports (Yue *et al.* 2018).

5.3.1.6 EIS Spectroscopy

PDA-$FeTiO_3$/GCE and $FeTiO_3$/GCE were electrochemically characterized using EIS. Nyquist plots for both electrodes were recorded at their OCV in the frequency range of 10^6 Hz to 1 Hz as shown in Figure 5.8. Comparing the impedance spectrum, PDA-$FeTiO_3$/GCE gave a larger value of R_{ct}, which might be owing to the polymer PDA layer on the nanostructures. The R_{ct} values obtained for $FeTiO_3$/GCE and PDA-$FeTiO_3$/GCE are 7105.00 Ω and 23089.00 Ω respectively. Also, the EIS spectrum are fitted with the equivalent circuit shown in the inset of Figure 5.8. PDA offers high resistance when coupled with $FeTiO_3$ nanostructure.

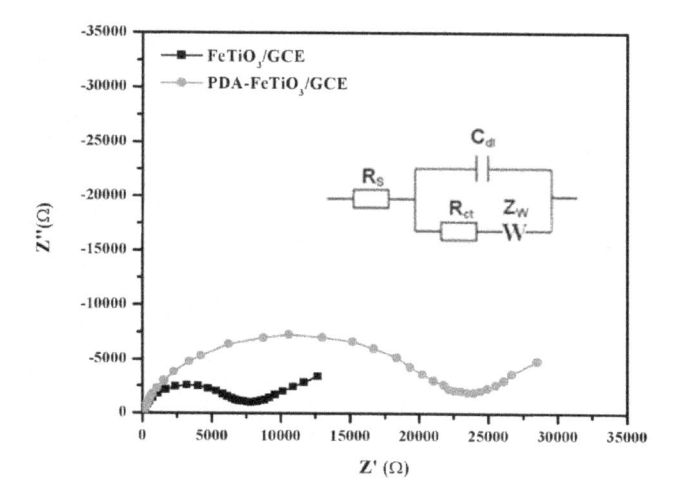

Figure 5.8. Nyquist Plot for FeTiO₃/GCE and PDA-FeTiO₃/GCE Recorded from a Solution of 0.1 M PBS and 5 mM K₄[Fe(CN)₆] in the Frequency Range of 10^6 Hz to 1 Hz

5.3.2 Electrocatalytic Activity of PDA-FeTiO₃/GCE

To demonstrate the electrocatalytic activity of PDA-FeTiO₃/GCE compared to FeTiO₃/GCE, CV curves were recorded in the potential range of -0.2 V to +0.8V. Figure 5.9 shows the CV curves for PDA-FeTiO₃/GCE and FeTiO₃/GCE at a scan rate of 100 mV s^{-1} in an electrolyte solution containing 0.1 mM DA and 1 M PBS. FeTiO₃/GCE showed an oxidation current of 2.80 µA and reduction current of 0.95 µA whereas, the PDA-FeTiO₃/GCE showed an oxidation current of 3.80 µA and reduction current of 2.43 µA. The peak currents were comparatively higher for PDA-FeTiO₃/GCE compared to FeTiO₃/GCE. Also, the peaks are well defined in case of the electrode modified with PDA-FeTiO₃. Although PDA-FeTiO₃ nanocomposite showed high R_{ct} compared to FeTiO₃, they exhibited a good catalytic activity. This is attributed to the high surface area, presence of functional groups on PDA and easy ion accessibility of the composite.

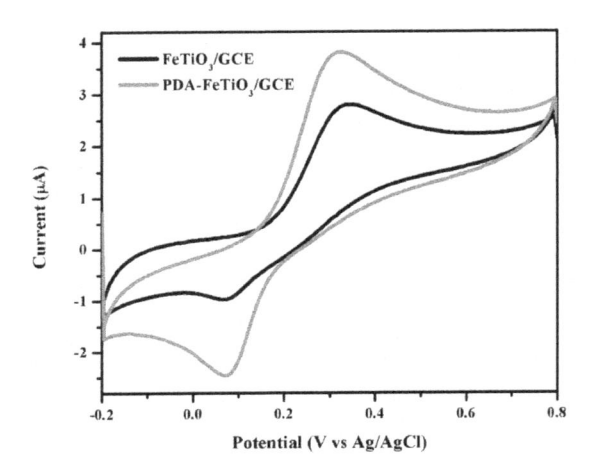

Figure 5.9. Cyclic Voltammogramm Depicting the Response of DA on FeTiO$_3$/GCE and PDA-FeTiO$_3$/GCE from a Solution of 0.1 M PBS and 0.1 mM of DA at a Scan Rate of 100 mV s^{-1}

Further, the effect of scan rate was studied on PDA-FeTiO$_3$/GCE as shown in Figure 5.10a. The CV curves were recorded at scan rates ranging from 100 mV s^{-1} to 1000 mV s^{-1} in 0.1 mM DA and 0.1 M PBS. The redox couple of DA showed an increase in peak current with increase in scan rate and a linear calibration plot between peak current and scan rate was obtained as shown in Figure 5.10b. This shows that oxidation of DA is an adsorption controlled process. The linear regression equation obtained was as follows.

I_{pa}=0.002 v(mVs^{-1}) + 3.56 (R^2= 0.9839) ; I_{pc}=-0.004 v(mVs^{-1}) + 2.33 (R^2= 0.9881)

(5.1)

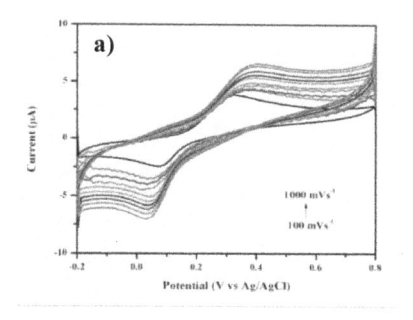

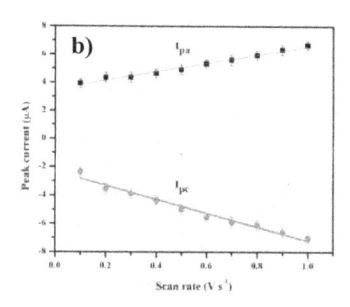

Figure 5.10. (a) CV Response of PDA-FeTiO₃/GCE for 0.1 mM DA at Different Scan Rates and (b) the Corresponding Calibration Plot

5.3.3 pH Study

As indicated earlier the oxidation of DA is dependent on pH of the electrolyte. CV studies were carried out for oxidation of DA at different pH ranging from 3 to 11 on PDA-FeTiO₃/GCE. Figure 5.11a shows the CV response at pH of 3, 5, 7, 9 and 11. The oxidation peak current of DA at pH 7 was higher compared to other pH. Also, the peak potential separation was less which indicates fast electron transfer at this pH. Figure 5.11b shows the variation of peak current with anodic peak potential (E_{pa}) and anodic peak current (I_{pa}). The linear regression equation was obtained as E_{Pa} (V) = 0.796 − 0.052 pH (R^2 = 0.8270). The slope of the graph was found to be 52 mV/pH which is close to the theoretical value of 59 mV per change in pH. This suggests the oxidation of DA is a two proton coupled two electron process.

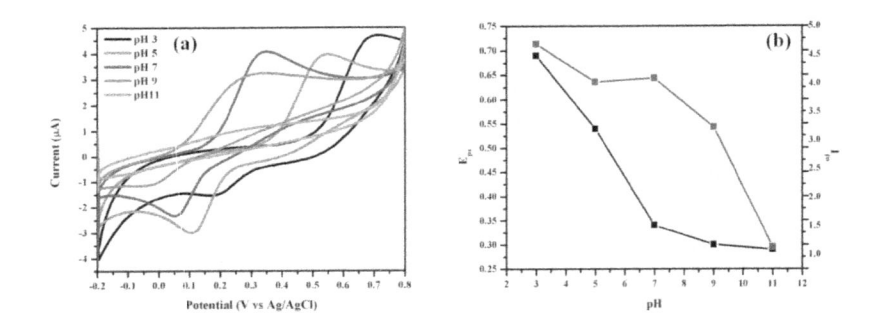

Figure 5.11. (a) CV Curves for 0.1 mM DA on PDA-FeTiO$_3$/GCE at a pH Range of 3 to 11 from a 0.1 M PBS Solution and (b) the Variation of E_{pa} and I_{pa} with Respect to pH

5.3.4 Sensing of DA and UA

DPV, a sensitive technique was employed for the detection of DA and UA. The DPV curves were recorded on PDA-FeTiO$_3$/GCE for various concentrations of DA ranging from 50 µM to 250 µM as shown in Figure 5.12a and their calibration plot is given in Figure 5.12b. A linear plot for peak current vs. their corresponding concentration was obtained. The peak currents increased linearly with DA concentrations and in a similar manner, the detection of UA was also performed by PDA-FeTiO$_3$/GCE as shown in Figure 5.12c and Figure 5.12d shows the linear calibration plot. The linear regression equations are

For DA, $I_{pa} = 0.003 (C_{DA}) + 0.18$ ($R^2 = 0.9841$) (5.2)

For UA, $I_{pa} = 0.002 (C_{UA}) + 0.21$ ($R^2 = 0.9978$) (5.3)

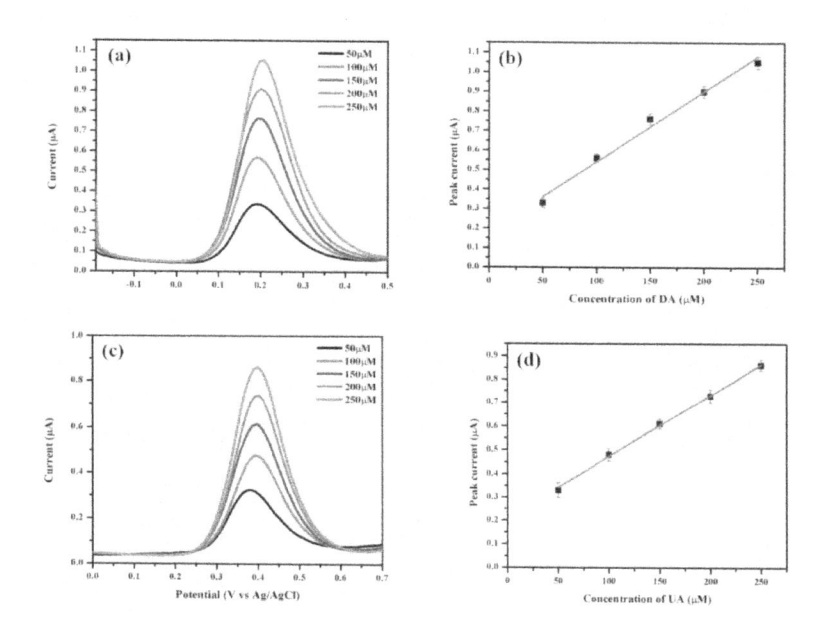

Figure 5.12. DPV Curves for (a) DA (50 µM to 250 µM) and (c) UA (50 µM to 250 µM) on PDA-FeTiO₃/GCE from a Solution of 0.1 M PBS and (b), (d) shows the Corresponding Calibration Plot

From the DPV curves, the limit of detection (LOD) and linear concentration ranges were calculated. LOD of 0.30 µM and 4.61 µM respectively for DA and UA and linear ranges from 50 µM to 250 µM for both DA and UA was estimated. The sensitivity calculated from the slope of the calibration plot was found to be 0.051 µA µM^{-1} cm^{-2} and 0.037 µA µM^{-1} cm^{-2} for DA and UA respectively. A comparison on the performance of the proposed sensor with different polymer based DA biosensors is given in Table 5.1. It is found that compared to FeTiO₃, the PDA-FeTiO₃ provided a high detection limit however it showed a long linear range compared to other electrodes such as SnO₂/AuNPs/PDA-RGO/GCE (Cui *et al.* 2017) and GCE/Cu^{2+}@PDA-MWCNTs (Shahbakhsh *et al.* 2018).

Table 5.1. A Comparative Performance of Various Polymer based DA Biosensors

S. No	Electrode	Linear Range (µM)	Limit of Detection (µM)	Ref
1	CPE-PPy/CuO	0.060-20, 20-1000	0.02	(Sheikh-Mohseni et al. 2016)
2	GCE/PANI-ZnO	0.2-2.4	0.015	(Fayemi et al. 2018)
3	GCE/PANI-NiO	0.2-2.4	0.016	(Fayemi et al. 2018)
4	GCE/PANI-Fe$_3$O$_4$	0.2-2.4	0.017	(Fayemi et al. 2018)
5	ZnO/PANI/RGO	0.001-1, 1-1000	0.0008	(Ghanbari et al. 2016)
6	ZnO–Cu$_x$O–PPy/GCE	0.1-130	0.04	(Ghanbari et al. 2015)
7	PPy-Ag-PVP/GCE	0.01-0.09	0.0126	(Vellaichamy et al. 2017)
8	SnO$_2$/AuNPs/PDA-RGO/GCE	0.008-20	0.005	(Cui et al. 2017)
9	Pdop@GR/MWCNTs	7.0-297	1.0	(Wang et al. 2016)
10	GCE/Cu^{2+}@PDA-MWCNTs	4.0-125	0.45	(Shahbakhsh et al. 2018)
11	PDA-FeTiO$_3$/GCE	50-250	0.3	Present work

CPE-carbon paste electrode, PPy-polypyrrole, RGO-reduced graphene oxide,

PANI-polyaniline, Pdop-polydopamine, GR-graphene

5.3.5 Selective and Simultaneous Detection of DA and UA

As mentioned, UA coexists with DA in biological fluids and also oxidizes at a potential similar to that of DA. Hence, the selectivity of PDA-FeTiO$_3$/GCE was carried out in the presence of UA. Herein, UA concentration was kept constant at 50 µM and DA concentration was varied from 100 µM to 500 µM. Figure 5.13a shows the DPV curves recorded on PDA-FeTiO$_3$/GCE and the calibration plot between DA concentration and peak current is shown in Figure 5.13b. Figure 5.13c depicts the DPV curves recorded using PDA-FeTiO$_3$/GCE for 50 µM DA and UA concentration from 100 µM to 500 µM. The two well defined peaks for DA and UA indicates that the sensor selectively detects DA in presence of UA. The corresponding calibration plot is given in Figure 5.13d. The linear regression equations for DA and UA are I_{pa}=0.002 (C_{DA}) + 0.277 (R^2= 0.9823) and I_{pa}=0.002 (C_{UA}) + 0.203 (R^2= 0.9910) respectively.

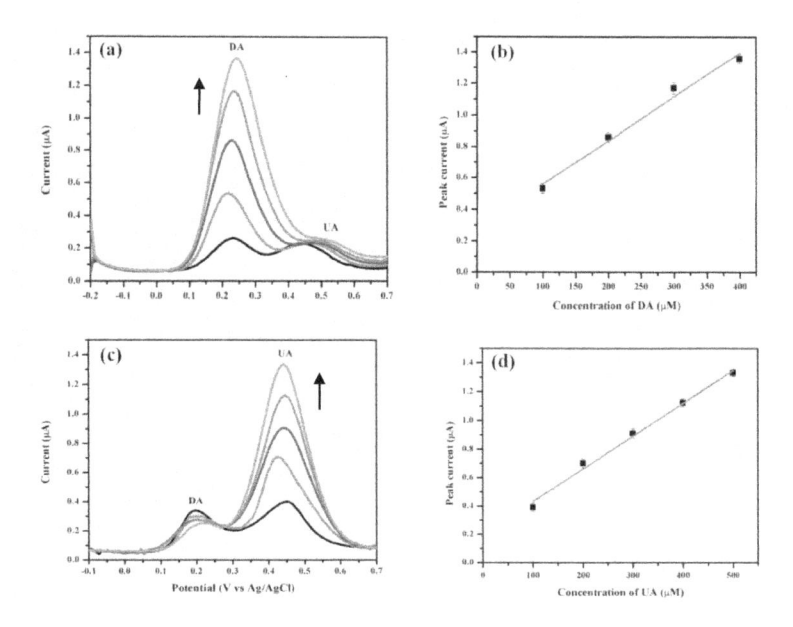

Figure 5.13. DPV Responses on PDA-FeTiO$_3$/GCE in 0.1 M PBS at Different Concentrations of (a) DA (100 µM to 500 µM), (c) UA (100 µM to 50c0 µM) and (b, d) their Corresponding Calibration Curves

Further to demonstrate the simultaneous detection, DA and UA were added successively in 0.1 M PBS electrolyte. The DPV analysis on PDA-FeTiO$_3$/GCE for DA and UA were done in concentrations ranging from 50 µM to 250 µM as given in Figure 5.14a. Their calibration plots are given in

Figure 5.14(b and c) respectively with the linear regression equations as
I_{pa}=0.003 (C_{DA}) + 0.23 (R^2= 0.9832) and I_{pa}=0.003 (C_{UA}) + 0.06 (R^2= 0.9950).

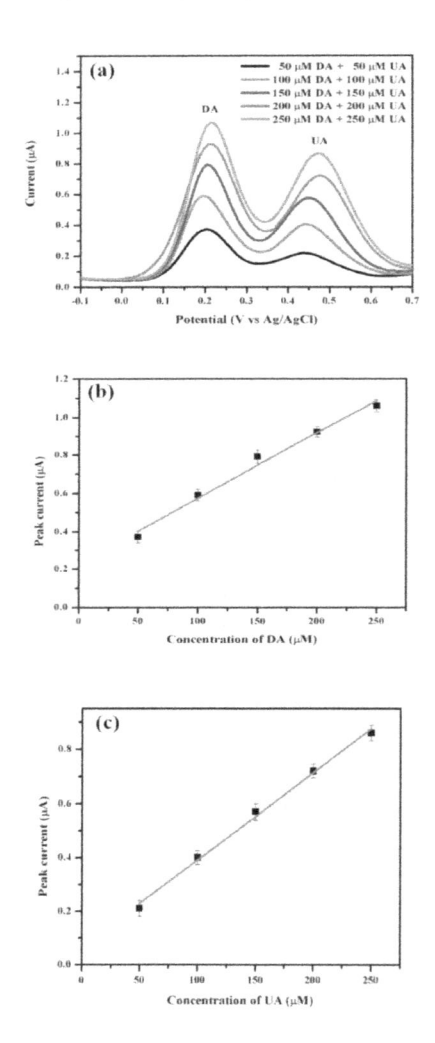

Figure 5.14. (a) DPV Response for Simultaneous Detection of DA and UA for Various Concentrations on PDA-FeTiO₃/GCE in 0.1 M PBS and (b) & (c) their Corresponding Calibration Plots

A detailed interference study with several other interferents such as glucose, urea, KNO$_3$, KCl, (NH$_4$)$_2$SO$_4$, FeSO$_4$, hydroxylamine and CuCl$_2$ was also studied using DPV and a bar plot showing the peak currents of the interferents is given in Figure 5.15. No significant change in the peak current of DA was observed in the presence of interfering agents. The PDA-FeTiO$_3$/GCE sensor was also used in the detection of AA. Though the sensor could detect AA, its performance towards detection of AA in the presence of DA was not so satisfactory. The oxidation peaks of DA and AA overlapped together at higher concentrations of AA. The stability of PDA-FeTiO$_3$/GCE was studied by successive measurements of the DA oxidation peak current in a solution of 0.1 mM DA. The sensor was stored in PBS buffer solution and tested for three week in an interval of two days. The sensor retained 84% of the initial current after 3 weeks which indicates good stability of the electrode.

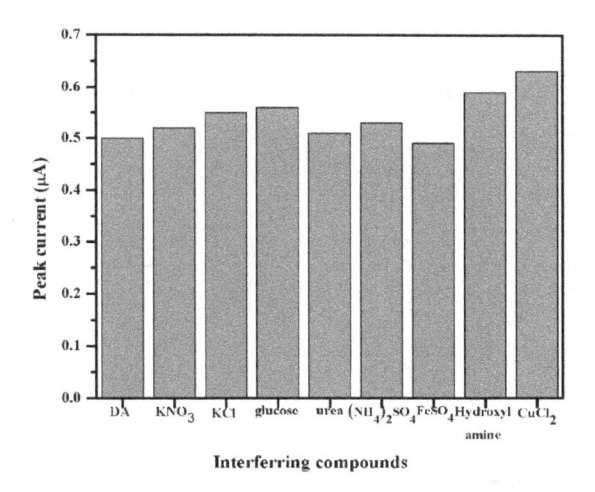

Figure 5.15. Bar Plot Depicting the Variation of Peak Current for DA Detection in Presence of Various Interfering Agents

5.3.6 Real Sample Analysis

The estimation of DA and UA in serum sample was studied using DPV. The electrolyte solution was 0.1 M PBS containing 100 µM serum. Known amount of DA and UA was added to the electrolyte and the oxidation current obtained was compared with the calibration plot obtained in Figure 5.12b. The following formula was used to calculate the recovery percentage.

$$\% \text{ of recovery} = C_{predicted}/C_{added} \times 100 \qquad (5.4)$$

The recovery values obtained were satisfactory ranging from 80% to 91% for DA in serum samples and the standard deviation was also very less. The recovery values for DA and UA in serum sample are provided in Table 5.2.

Table 5.2. DA and UA Estimation in Human Biological Samples using PDA-FeTiO₃/GCE

	Amount of DA added (µM)	Amount of DA predicted (µM)	% of recovery	Amount of UA added (µM)	Amount of UA predicted (µM)	% of recovery
Serum	80	64.38	80.47±1	80	60.47	75.58±2
	160	145.74	91.08±3	160	134	83.75±1
	240	214.77	89.48±2	240	195.46	81.44±1

5.4 SUMMARY

PDA coated FeTiO₃ nanocomposites were synthesized by a simple procedure and are characterized using SEM, TEM, XRD, FTIR and XPS respectively. From CV, the electro-oxidation of DA was studied and the PDA-FeTiO₃/GCE showed better activity compared to FeTiO₃/GCE. Further, the detection of DA and UA was carried out using DPV and a low detection limit of 0.3 µM was observed for DA. No interference from UA was seen which suggested the excellent selectivity of the sensor towards DA. The stability of the sensor was tested and showed to retain 84% of the initial value. Finally, the sensor was validated in biological human serum sample. The PDA-FeTiO$_3$/GCE sensor was shown to be promising in terms of selectivity, sensitivity and stability. It is inferred that the PDA coating offered improved stability to the sensor compared to bare FeTiO$_3$.

CHAPTER 6

CONCLUSIONS AND FUTURE SCOPE

The development of electrochemical sensor with low detection limit, good selectivity, high sensitivity and stability is challenging. In the case of electrochemical detection of DA, the sensor should exhibit sub-micromolar detection limit (present in human body), selective towards DA in presence of UA/AA and long term stability. For the present investigation, perovskite nanostructure was chosen and they exhibit high catalytic activity due to the presence of Fe and Ti in multiple oxidation state together with the presence of oxygen deficient sites and high surface area of the nanostructure.

A summary of the major contributions of the investigation is as follows. Chapter 3 dealt with electrochemical detection of DA using GCE electrode modified with $FeTiO_3$ ($FeTiO_3$/GCE). The $FeTiO_3$/GCE showed good electrocatalytic performance for DA oxidation with anodic and cathodic peak current of 2.80 µA and 0.95 µA respectively. DPV studies were also carried out for both DA and UA, wherein much lower detection limits such as 1.3nM and 30nM were observed respectively. The LOD values reported are the lowest among earlier reported perovskite based DA sensors. The sensor also showed a wide linear range for both DA and UA, which also highlights the superiority of the sensor in terms of performance.

Further to understand the mechanistic pathway for DA oxidation the electrochemical kinetic investigation was carried out. Chapter 4 entirely dealt with the study of DA electrochemistry with the use of electrochemical experiments such as hydrodynamic voltammetry and impedance spectroscopy. The mechanistic pathway for FeTiO$_3$/GCE was found to be similar to that of bare GCE and the reaction was two electron coupled two proton transfer process. Though a similar pathway was seen, the kinetics of FeTiO$_3$/GCE was slower. High intramolecular cyclization was noted at alkaline pH with the formation of melanin-like compound. And also, due to passivation the R_{ct} was higher with increasing potentials.

Chapter 5 highlights the enhancement in the stability of the sensor when a polymer like PDA was coated on the FeTiO$_3$ nanostructure. The PDA was obtained by polymerization of DA in tris buffer at a pH of 8.4. The CV results showed comparatively higher peak currents for PDA-FeTiO$_3$/GCE than FeTiO$_3$/GCE. However, when the PDA-FeTiO$_3$/GCE was employed for DA detection by DPV, the detection limit of DA was found to be 0.3 µM which is higher than that of FeTiO$_3$/GCE. This may be due to the increased electron transfer resistance as inferred from the impedance spectroscopy. However the sensor showed good stability upto 3 weeks by retaining 84% of the peak current. The results inferred that the nanocomposite improved the performance of the DA sensor in terms of sensitivity and selectivity although by compromising the detection limit.

6.1 FUTURE PERSPECTIVES

In this study the performance of perovskite nanostrucuture in the detection of DA was investigated. The detection limit inferred from the sensing studies indicated that, DA can be detected upto sub-micromolar concentration range using FeTiO$_3$ which is equivalent to the physiological level present in human body. However the electrode exhibited poor stability. The electrochemistry of DA on FeTiO$_3$ also suggested sluggish electron transfer kinetics. The challenge was overcome by introducing a polymer coated nanocomposite (PDA-FeTiO$_3$)

which enhanced the stability of the sensor however by compromising the sensitivity and detection limit. Hence from this analysis it seems that, there is lot of scope for improvement in the performance of the sensor. This can be approached in two ways either by inducing functional groups on the $FeTiO_3$ nanostructure to improve its stability or the coating thickness of the polymer (PDA) can be optimized to improve the detection limit by reducing R_{ct}. In addition the electron transfer kinetics can also be improved which in turn enhance the sensitivity of the sensor. Further scope of improvement lies in device fabrication or in other words to develop a prototype of DA sensor using $FeTiO_3$. However, it needs to overcome several challenges so as to realize its commercial success.